DESPERADO
A True Story of Redemption by God's Amazing Grace

Kenneth M. James

Desperado:
A True Story of Redemption by God's Amazing Grace

Copyright © 2022 by Kenneth James

All rights are reserved. Printed in the United States of America. No part of this book may be reproduced, stored in a retrieval system, transmitted (electronic, mechanical, photocopy, recording) or otherwise without the prior written permission of the copyright holder, except as permitted by US copyright law. Unless otherwise notated scripture references are from the King James Version of the Bible

For information contact:
Kenneth James
Email: **kenj1944@att.net**

ISBN: 979844700947 2

Published By:
Emmanuel Writing Services
ews.publish@gmail.com

Endorsements

Our cousin, Kenneth James, once lived the fast and egregious life of a streetwise criminal. Intimidation and violence were his creed. His life was profoundly changed by the power of a real encounter with the Gospel of Jesus Christ. Elder James' riveting life story of surrender and answering God's call to ministry is told in this powerful and intriguing book, Desperado. We encourage everyone to read and be inspired by the story of this remarkable, authentic story of one man's bold faith and witness for God's redemptive love, and power to save anyone.
      Pastors Victor and Elder Nancy McCullough, Elders
      The United Methodist Church, Oklahoma

Desperado is the rite-of-passage-read for every young person matriculating into adulthood. A modern day Damascus-Road-Experience, this epic account of one man's redemptive journey is gripping and inspiring to say the least. Desperado dispels myths that glamorize gangster lifestyle and re-defines the crown of the *Old-G*. It is transparent, honest, and compelling.
      Joy A. Lewis, Host,
      The Review with Joy & Company Radio Show

I highly recommend this book for everyone. It is a testimony to the life changing power of Jesus Christ. I saw firsthand the God-change in this man—he is my father.
      Valeicyia Houston

Kenneth James is a true man of God and one of the most effective communicators in the Christian world today.
>Royce Hall,
TDCJ-CVCA, National Advisor
ALPHAUSA Prisons & Reentry

I am excited to recommend this book, Evangelist James testimony is for these times. He is a faithful servant of God. I serve with him in prison ministry. A must buy book to be shared with the world.
>Missionary T. Dabney
State Approved Prison Volunteer

To Elder Kenneth James:
Congratulations on your perseverance, and new accomplishments. We can truly say we are very proud of you as a brother-in-law for over fifty-two years and a faithful, dedicated church member. We thank God for you! Love
>Pastor & Lady F. Sheppard

Table of Contents

In the Beginning 13

South Dallas 17

The U S Army 23

Back Home 28

The Sheppard Family 31

The Road to Perdition 36

The Hand of God 47

Freedom 49

My Damascus Road Experience 63

Freedom Again 65

The War 67

Continuation 74

Road to Redemption 76

Road to Restoration 82

Inside Restoration 95

The Final Test Before Home 99

Inner Change Freedom Initiative 103

Maturing In Christ 105

Home 111

Re-Entry 113

Moving Forward 115

Dedication

I would like to dedicate this book to my lovely wife, Shar'Ron James. We were divorced and I was alienated from her for twelve years, because of my criminal lifestyle. She obeyed the voice of God, while I was yet in prison, and allowed me to reenter her life as her husband.

Shar'Ron is a strong woman of God, tailored by the hand of God for me only. She is a woman of conviction and faith. She is filled with the wisdom of God. Her parents, Reverend Waco Sheppard and Louise Sheppard instilled in her the principles of Christ by being an example of godliness in their marriage. I thank God for her every day; we have been in each other's life since 1964. It is through the Grace of God and the love of Shar'Ron, I have weathered many storms, trials, and tribulations.

When you read this book, Shar'Ron plays a big part behind the scenes in the making of my story. The Lord has blessed me to write this book for His Glory.

Shar'Ron, you are my rock, my best friend, and my greatest critic (in a good way). Thank God for His amazing grace in all areas of my life. God is a restorer of the broken life, home, marriage, and any relationship.

I am a living testimony of His redemption. We are a living testimony of his agape love.

Shar'Ron Sheppard

Whoso findeth a wife findeth a good thing, and obtaineth favour of the Lord.
Provervs 18:22 KJV

To Our Children:

I also dedicate this book to my daughter, Valeicyia Houston and my son, Kenneth Smith.

Valeicyia was 4 years old when Shar'Ron and I were married on Oct. 30, 1967. I never abused my family physically, but the emotional abuse and mental trauma I caused as I lived a criminal lifestyle would be immeasurable had it not been for God's grace. Valeicyia is a woman of God, and yes, she forgives me and loves me like I was there for her 100%.

Kenneth was born in 1964. He saw my criminal lifestyle up close, and yet he loves me and forgives me to this day, just as if I was there for him 100%. God healed our relationship.

I truly thank God for them both, along with my mom, the late Pearl James, who the Lord allowed to see me transformed from a career criminal to a man serving God.

God restored my broken relationships.

But God!
With deep gratitude — Kenneth James

Lo, children are an heritage of the LORD: and the fruit of the womb is his reward.

[4] As arrows are in the hand of a mighty man; so are children of the youth.

[5] Happy is the man that hath his quiver full of them: they shall not be ashamed, but they shall speak with the enemies in the gate. Psalm 127: 3-5 KJV

Preface

This book is the direct inspiration of God's Holy Spirit. It is a testament of the glory of God and His Amazing Grace. It is my desire to encourage those who are struggling with addictions of any sort, to show the love of God even in a selfish, wicked world, and to give hope to a dying world mired in hopelessness, hatred and sin.

This is a true story of a man who experienced God's amazing grace. With respect to those living and deceased discretion was at the forefront of this project. This is not a novel, one of the classics, or a story of folly. It is the true life story of my rise and fall in the drug culture and gangster-like lifestyle. It is the good, bad, and the ugly of my life before and after Christ. To experience the full impact of this story, please read the fifth chapter of the book of Mark in the Holy Bible whichever version is your preference.

This book is written for all, believers and non-believers alike.

There is no depth of sin you can sink in, no act of sin you can commit, and no lifestyle you can have that God's amazing grace cannot reach. I pray you read with an open mind and that your soul is blessed.

In Christ,
Kenneth 'Unc' James

Introduction

Saul's Conversion Acts 9:1-6 (NIV)

Meanwhile, Saul was still breathing out murderous threats against the Lord's disciples. He went to the high priest and asked him for letters to the synagogues in Damascus, so that if he found any there who belonged to the Way, whether men or women, he might take them as prisoners to Jerusalem. As he neared Damascus on his journey, suddenly a light from heaven flashed around him. He fell to the ground and heard a voice say to him, "Saul, Saul, why do you persecute me?"
"Who are you, Lord?" Saul asked.
"I am Jesus, whom you are persecuting," he replied. "Now get up and to into the city, and you will be told what you must do."

Like Paul on the road to Damascus, I too have been redeemed.

In the early 1950's, the streets of North Dallas, like most American cities, provided few positive role models for rambunctious and inquisitive black boys. At that time, the only whites in the neighborhood were the grocery store owners. We were surrounded by adults who *existed* in survival mode. We were cornered by the strict rules of segregation and the religious taunting of those damning us to hell if we did not walk the straight and narrow.

I was one of those rambunctious and inquisitive black boys. I went from the streets of Dallas to the prison walls of state, federal, and military facilities to the life of a free, born-again Christian.

This is my Damascus Road Experience.

***

In The Beginning

I was born October 15, 1944, the firstborn to Ms. Pearl James, affectionately known as Sister-Baby. I was the first grandchild of Morey Page Ector, known as Doll Baby. My family, like most families in the 1950s, did not have much. Although that area has changed completely, through the lens of my memory, I vividly see every corner.

My lineage was of the Christian way. Our family was rooted in the Holiness Church. The patriarch, my great-grandfather, was Bishop E. M. Page of Page Temple Church of God in Christ, on the main drag of North Dallas—Thomas Avenue. It rested a few blocks from the infamous center of all kinds of street action—Thomas and Hall Streets.

Temple Church of God in Christ was a prominent staple in the community. I attended this church until roughly twelve years old. My great-grandfather and his wife Mollie Woods Page, known as Momma Page, were well respected by blacks and whites for their Christian lives. They ensured that we attended church service if nothing else. As children, we were expected to recite book, chapter, and verse of what seemed like every scripture. We endured because the elders readily gave us treats for trying.

For fun, some of us rambunctious boys would emulate the grown-ups and pretend we got caught up in the spirit. We were chastised by the first ready-hand. A reminder that it takes a village to raise children.

I never knew my father or any of his people.

When I was born, my mother lived with Doll Baby along with my Aunts Helen, Mollie, and Marcelene. They were working toward their future, neither had children. My mother was going to nursing school at St Paul Hospital. For two years, I was the only child in the house, spoiled rotten. And then my sister Barbara J. James was born. Two years later, Zoe Ann James was born. We were one big happy family in the big house at 2606 State Street. We did not have much, but we ate well. Holidays were special.

I was raised in a house that was void of men folk. All my uncles had moved out of town. I enjoyed my pals in our neighborhood. My grandmother and aunts kept me involved in stuff for boys through the YMCA and the Boy Scotts. I can recall feeling resentment at times for the lack of males to look up to. I needed some positive male influence in my life. The feeling however was readily over-shadowed by the joy of hanging out with my pals in our neighborhood.

My Mother graduated from St. Paul's School of Nursing and got hired for the graveyard shift at Parkland Hospital.

My sisters and I were put to bed at 10:00 p.m. before she left for work, and she called us at 6:00 a.m. to get ready for school. She got home at 8:00 a.m., combed my sister's hair, dressed us, fed us, and sent us off to school. I was in the first grade, Barbara was in the second grade, and Zoe was attending St. John's Baptist Church kindergarten. In an all-black community like North Dallas, *the village* raised the children—for real. My sisters and I left for school holding hands, we dropped Zoe at St. John's, and Barbara and I proceeded to our school, J.W. Ray Elementary.

Elementary school years were typical. Occasionally something out of the ordinary happened like when Aunt Mollie married Ernie Banks of the Chicago Cubs. There were also the issues of the government-built shotgun houses, the projects and busing which kept residents in black communities on a ledge one way or the other.

TEACHABLE MOMENTS

Redeemed by the Blood of Jesus

The typical two-parent household is no longer the standard for the makeup of our family dynamics which changes from household to household. The Bible places great emphasis on genealogy, family dynamics and lineage. This allows God to show the historical accuracy of His Word, and we see God using anyone and everyone to work miraculously on our behalf for His glory.

Regardless of your family's dynamics, God can turn something fragmented and dysfunctional into a beautiful work of art for His glorious purpose.

"You don't choose your family. They are God's gift to you, as you are to them."
Desmond Tutu

South Dallas

In 1956, my grandmother bought a house in South Dallas. She convinced my mother to let us live with her in the new white neighborhood. Mother agreed, and once again we all lived in the big house with Aunt Marcelene, her daughter, and occasional visits from her husband, Uncle Cliff, who lived in Longview after he accepted a coaching position at the black high school there. *Jim Crow* was alive and prevalent, and even though there was a school a couple of blocks from the house, we walked twenty-five blocks to Phyllis Wheatley Elementary school along with all the other kids whose parents were trying to better themselves.

We transitioned from elementary school to middle school. I was a consistent A/B student through the ninth grade. The family's aspiration for me was law school. Hoping for another Thurgood Marshall I suppose. However, change is and inevitable concept. The all-white Forest Avenue High School was gifted to the blacks in South Dallas. As education and opportunities took a step up, so did the street mischief.

My transition from elementary to middle school was a step into the world of gangsters, thugs and all things daring. I was intrigued by the mafia dealings I read about in newspapers. I idolized Albert Anastasia, also known as The One-Man Army. He was an Italian-American mobster, hit man, and crime boss. He was one of the founders of the modern American Mafia and eventually rose to the position of boss in what became the modern Gambino crime family. He was my idol— the lord high executioner of gangland.

I hung out in the park with the older thugs. I took sips of thunderbird wine after school and went home practically drunk. Oh, I was fussed at, but that did not bother me. I was raised by women with three sisters and four girl cousins. We all got along, but really a house with all girls. I was my own man. There was no male figure around to put or keep me in check. By no means does this excuse my behavior—I made the choices.

James Madison High School is where my life as a thug took off on another scale. By the time I entered high school, I was well known throughout South Dallas and not as the choir-boy mind you. My guardians did their best to steer me on a good path, but I made choices that shattered my family's expectations of me. Though many of my friends from high school chose differently and became successful in their careers, I chose to become like my idol, an enforcer who would execute violence for a price.

By age fifteen, I was ruling the streets. I was groomed by the older high school drop-outs in the hood. Some had been to prison already and earned their badge of honor for doing so. They taught me the streets. I did not drop out of school, but my grades dropped. I stayed out until ten or eleven o'clock at night. My grandmother would get on my case, but I paid her no mind.

The summer after my ninth-grade school year, I was initiated into *the clique (w*e did not call ourselves *a gang* back in the fifties). It was a typical summer night. Residuals from the day's high temperature left many seated on front porches with large jars of iced water, tea or beer.

18

Gingham curtains swayed rhythmically through open windows. Young women were posed with hands on their hip as they perused the streets yelling for younger siblings to come home. A mix of pulsating beats, smooth crooners, and down-home dirty blues filled the air. We walked the streets of South Dallas as though we had no cares in the world; absorbing the sights and sounds of a hot summer's night. My mission was to "Jaw" the first male we encountered. In other words, I was just to walk up to him, hit him in the jaw, and the rest of the fellas would jump in, easy enough. I was nervous that I would not pass the test. I did, and the fellas let the whole school know—I was one of them. I did not care about my guardian's disapproval or how much they got on my case. This was the path I willfully chose.

It was the summer of '59. The country was preparing to enter a new decade. Frankie Lymon and the Teenagers' popular song, I'm not a Juvenile Delinquent, was still climbing the charts and I was busy building my "rep" as one to be feared in South Dallas. I was good with my fist, a knife, and I was always ready for a squabble. I enjoyed inflicting pain and fear. With my eyes fixated on Albert Anastasia and the like, I was well on my way to being kingpin. This was the summer I was introduced to drugs.

Secobarbitals, a controlled substance known as Reds on the streets, were my introduction into the drug culture. The one-dollar-little-red pill was a downer—a sedative taken by mouth or mainlining—intravenous injection.

I was in tenth grade, enrolled at James Madison high school for attendance only. "Bussing" was in full throttle. Students were bused from the Oak Cliff section of Dallas, West Dallas area, and from all over Dallas.

At one time James Madison had a student body close to 2000 and the atmosphere was ripe everyday for a fight. It was Oak Cliff against South Dallas, West Dallas against East Dallas. North Dallas was not drawn in because their black students went to the old Booker T. Washington High School, the oldest high school in Dallas for Blacks. Also, in South Dallas was Lincoln High School in a cutthroat part of town called Boonton.

Usually everybody had a girlfriend in their part of town. If a boy from South Dallas went to see a girl in Oak Cliff, he was liable to get beat up. I was determined to be the one respected in every part of Dallas, especially in every city park.

At the age of seventeen, I started my quest, with four others who also craved that feeling of being respected, along with counting all the girls we could get. We knew it was not going to be easy. We could be hurt, killed, or sent to the joint (prison). We didn't care; it was all about establishing a reputation. So in the summer, when girls threw parties in their back yards, and we heard about it—we turned the party out. In other words, we started the fight. If anybody had a complaint or a threat to get even, we took the fight to them, no matter where they lived.

I was drinking, getting high off the reds, and valos which were the common name for Benzodiazepines in the fifties. I did not care for weed (marijuana), I was still lat home, going to school, and disrupting school. I had not started on heroin and cocaine yet.

After I solidified my status in South Dallas, I moved to North Dallas to live with my great Aunt Rebecca and transferred to Booker T. Washington, where I would join the classmates I knew from first to sixth grade in North Dallas before we moved to South Dallas.

I was expelled indefinitely from Booker T. and sent back to James Madison. In order to be re-enrolled in Madison, I had to meet with the Dean of students.

Well, about fifteen minutes into the meeting, I told the dean in a not so nice way what she could do with her precious Madison. I then went to Lincoln High School where I had more enemies than friends, not to enroll, but to squabble. Two of the fellas were with me and we had an old fashioned donnybrook brawl. There were times I had to get somewhere — get run off. I got what I set out to get — a rep and my grandmother and aunts, stopped trying to set me right.

TEACHABLE MOMENTS

Redeemed by the Blood of Jesus

I was not raised with the wealth of this world; my family brought me up in the principles of the bible. The love I experienced from my family was wonderful. We were not the perfect American family portrayed on TV like Ozzie and Harriett or Father Knows Best, but even in the absence of a male role model, my grandmother, mother, and aunts loved us.

Our family worshiped the Lord during challenging times. My sisters and I loved each other as we enjoyed one another in our younger years of growing up in meager times. Our foundation was LOVE.

No matter what your current condition in life is now; you can find comfort in the memories of your childhood. I know that some families are toxic, but you were still in God`s love and the responsibilities of children lies upon the guardians. From this teachable moment comes the lesson that regardless of your family dynamics, you choose what path you will take when you reach the age of accountability. I chose the path of destruction. Today, you can choose the path of life.
Prayerfully read and meditate on the following scriptures:
Ephesians 6:1-4, Rom.6:12
Prov.22:6, St. Luke 15:11-12

Joshua 24:14-17, Acts 3:19

***
The U. S. Army

Nineteen sixty two rolled in and I had the girls, the respect, and John F. Kennedy was my president. I decided to do what my grandmother had been preaching for me to do—go to the Army.InFeb.1963I went to the Army recruiter in downtown Dallas and joined the U S Army.
I took a good look at President John F. Kennedy during the cold war between Russia and the U.S. and liked what I saw in him. I was sworn in the U.S. Army March of 1962. I was bused to Fort Polk, La. for basic training, along with a hundred others. I was excited about being a soldier, and accomplishing something positive in my life.

After arriving in Fort Polk, and settling into the army way of life, I was slapped in my face with the reality of racism in the U.S. Army. I noticed that blacks did more KP duty in the kitchen than whites. Blacks pulled the late night and early morning (1am-5am) guard duty. We tried to meet with the company commander about the problem, but we always ended up with the 1st Sergeant.

Halfway through boot camp, one night we were in our barracks (though integrated, the spirit of racism was prevalent) cleaning our rifles. A white boy from Wisconsin called me the "N" word. My rifle was broke down to clean all the parts as we were taught. The bayonet was on my bunk next to where I was sitting. Seeing red as he called me that, I jumped up, grabbed my bayonet by the hilt and flipped it where I had it by the blade. If I had used the blade, I would have killed him, so I used the handle to beat him to a bloody pulp. I took South Dallas all the way to Fort Polk.

The M.P.s came and arrested me, I went to the guardhouse where I was detained before my court martial. After three days, I was brought to court and was sentenced to six months with no pay ,restricted to the barracks, no weekend pass, and clean up detail all over the post where needed. Well, I had made up my mind that I was not going to go fight a stranger and my own countrymen could not get over racism in the Armed Forces of America.

The men got paid, I did not, and as they cleaned up that Friday night to go on their weekend pass, I had a plan.

To execute my plan I needed $10.00 for a bus ticket back to Dallas on the old Continental Trailways Bus. I started a crap game, and the blacks egged the whites into it, before long I had $20.00. I had my bus fare, now I needed to get off the base. I could not leave the base for any reason. With my gangster attitude, as the bus loaded up in front of our barracks to take them into Leesville, La. - five miles, I boarded the bus knowing that the M.P.s would come aboard to check for weekend passes .No pass—off the bus. I sat in the back of the bus with no pass. M.P.s boarded to check passes. Two seats before they got to me, their walkie-talkie came alive for them in an emergency. They jumped off the bus, told the bus driver to go onto town and I was on my way to big "D". I knew I was going A.W.O.L. (absent without leave). I felt exhilaration within my soul. I screwed the mighty U.S. Army!

I got off the base bus, waited an hour and when I finally boarded the bus to Dallas, I sailed on in with a fifth of Thunderbird wine in my hand. It took about five hours with all the stops to get to Dallas.

Once I arrived in Dallas, I went to my girlfriend's house. She was amazed and afraid. I went to the streets and greeted all my peers with the realization that I left the Army without their permission .All the addresses that I gave the recruiter I did not go to them, because I knew-that they would be coming after me. I was going to party and do what I did best — raise hell! I knew if they tried to put me back on active duty, I would run like a jack rabbit.

The Viet Nam war was in its early stage and I was not going, I had made up my mind that I would go to prison before I went over there to fight a people I knew nothing about. You got to remember that the *good-old* U.S.A. was segregated. No civil rights prevailed. Blacks sat in the back of the city buses, and went to the back door of restaurants. The diners blacks had were shacks. As a matter of fact, the part of Dallas called Deep Ellum, is a part of the Black culture. In the forties it was called Central Track— the down town area that blacks could call their own. We had the Harlem Theater, Gypsy Tea Room, and many more with historical significance.

I knew that they were coming after me, I did not care, I was going to get my partying on. I came home in April, 1963 and did my thing. I had no place of residence and just slept where I could. August, 1963, word came down the grapevine of the streets that the F.B.I. was in Dallas looking for me. It would be September before they apprehended me and I entered Dallas County Jail where I waited for the arrival of the M.P.s from Carswell Air Force Base in Fort Worth to pick me up. From there I would wait for the Military prison bus from Fort Hood to pick me up and take me to the stockade at Fort Hood where I would be tried for AWOL (absent without leave).

The process for my military court martial began once I arrived at Fort Hood, Texas. This would be my first taste of incarceration of any kind. I had been in the drunk- tank of city jail, but not in the county jail or the prison environment.

We were in two-man cells on a cell block of one hundred. September, 1963, I was evaluated by a psychologist, declared to have an anti-social personality. I did not say "sir" to the officers, and at my trial, I told everybody in the room; Generals, Colonels, and Majors, that if they send me back to active duty, I am running like a rabbit. Well, before the verdict came back onNovember23, 1963, we got the news that John F. Kennedy was shot in Dallas, Texas. After he died, the world was in shock, they let us go free and I came back to Dallas with a feather in my hat—I bucked the army. My reputation went up a notch or two; I was gaining street status as never before. I worked at odd jobs, living with my grandmother in South Dallas and sometimes with my mother.By1964, I was rolling. I began to live the life I thought was the good life.

TEACHABLE MOMENTS

Redeemed by the Blood of Jesus

My advice to anyone considering enlisting in the U.S. Armed Forces is to get a correct mindset. As you have read, my experience in the army was fueled by a corrupt mindset. Let your mindset reflect the principles of God's Word.

If you are not a believer in Christ Jesus, you still can have a mindset of moral priorities for your life, wherever you go, especially in the armed forces. The same evil of systemic racism that I encountered is alive and thriving today in the armed forces.
What can you do in such a situation in your life? The best advice that I can give you is not to conform to the ways of this world; you do that by making choices that line up with godly principals. Again, I encourage you to seek salvation through the gospel of Jesus Christ. I did not do that in 1963 when I was in the army.

Allow me to recommend Jesus to you, try Him. You will not regret it. Prayerfully read the following scripture Ephesians 4: 17-32.
You can do this; it is all a matter of choice, read Philippians 1:6 and 2:5.

***

Back Home

I returned to Dallas with a dishonorable discharge from the U.S. Army. I was ready to continue my life of chaotic behavior. My grandmother was disappointed in me, my mom had moved to South Dallas where my sisters moved with her down the street from my grandmother. My mom moved on the corner of Wendelkin and Lenway Streets. I moved in with my mother and sisters. Mama had all her children with her again, although we were older. My sister Barbara was a senior at Madison High School and working in a work/school program at the Neiman Marcus warehouse, where she stayed for fifty years as an employee after graduating high school. Zoe was still in high school and momma worked at Forest Avenue Hospital on Forest Avenue (now known as MLK Blvd). The baby girl, Lee Marilyn (Tiny) born June 4, 1957, was the center of attention at seven years old.

As for me, I was running the streets — building my rep, which was pretty well known by now. I lived part time with a girl, and had a son by the young lady down the street from us. I was drinking but not doing drugs. I did not care about the weed, not smoking it at least — I sold it. I got jobs bussing tables in various places, but quit after stealing money from many of them. I did not consider myself a gang leader but I was well respected by all.

In1964, I got arrested for getting caught with a gun (60days in county jail, 2year probation.) I continued on my path of destruction. That summer, a good friend of mine was killed in the Grand Avenue Oakland part of South Dallas (John Henry Brown School area). We unofficially divided South Dallas into territories.

No one could venture into a territory without the expressed permission of the parties ruling the streets for that territory. I was one of the few who had multiple-territory privilege. When my friend was shot and killed in the John Henry Brown school area, I had acquired two pistols and we (the Colonial Park clique) decided to bring street justice to the area. For three weeks we terrorized the area. Whether friend or foe, everyone knew Kenneth James as the enforcer. I stopped working and drank a lot. I hung out on the streets getting protection money from those who wanted to party in our area. That was my way of life in 1965.

By the time 1966 rolled in, I was dropping pills of all kinds, reds, valiums and others. Women who had prescriptions for these pills gladly sold them with our protection. A new night club, The Guthrie Club, opened on Ervay Street in South Dallas. This was the place to be on the weekends. Any kind of action you wanted was there. The gangs had an unwritten truce when at the club.

One night, I was drunk and was put out of the club. The police were called. I was taken to jail, and when I emptied my pockets, I pulled out two pills and my arresting charge was changed from drunk and disorderly conduct to possession of a controlled substance, I was sentenced to six months county jail time. In jail, you could run into friend or foe. However, all beefs were settled on the streets, not in jail; another unwritten code of the streets, because we were all trying to make the best of a bad situation.

While I was going in and out of jail, my family had no idea what was wrong with me. My Aunt Marcelene wanted me to submit to a psychiatric examination. Why? Because no other male in my family behaved like I did. When they came for a visit, I left. They were not there as a role model for me growing up, so I figured I have nothing to say to them.

To this day, I have not heard a thing from my biological dad his people or anyone. Maybe he had that inner rage in him that I carried for so many years. My family would not answer my questions about my dad; my older family members carried that secret to their graves with them.

I floated between my mom's house and the homes of the different young ladies I was with for a minute or two. I was breaking the law on all points, never getting caught.

***
The Sheppard Family

In the spring of 1967, my life made a dramatic change. I needed to take a break from the streets; I decided to "catch out" for a month or so. I would go to the employment office every day, not to get a real job (I did not want that) but I would get a temporary- one-day job and get paid the same day. We called that catching out. I got a job that would last a month paying every day. On that job I ran into an old friend, another person of the same character as me. We worked every day, and got paid, and did what we did. My friend told me his girlfriend, Margo, had a friend that he could introduce me to and the four of us could go to the club one Friday night. I always considered myself a playboy, who was not tied down to any one woman, but I had been burned on blind dates before, I went to Booker T. Washington with his friend Margo, so I said ok.

September of '67, on the Friday appointed, we got off work, and went to Margo's apartment to meet my blind date who was in the bedroom. When she came out to greet us; I was knocked off my feet for two reasons:

1. I knew her, she was the sister of my friend that was killed in the John Henry Brown School area in 1964, and I lost touch with the family after his death

2. She was the most beautiful sight I had ever seen, she completely stole my heart. She had blossomed into a beautiful young lady.

Her name was Shar'Ron Sheppard, I went to James Madison High with her— the little time I was there.
We had a mini reunion and we made plans to go out Saturday night. I could not drive and neither of us had a car, but we always had cab fare.

We were drinking at the club, enjoying friends and one another. The club was crowded to capacity, someone passed our table, stepped on my foot, kept walking and I went off (slang for fighting mad). I started a fight, my friend stood with me, so, we caught a cab back to where we started the night. Shar'Ron was upset, but she got over it. She knew the kind of life I lived. She stayed in my corner, cautiously, but she stayed.

I was living at my grandmother's house, every morning at six, I called Shar'Ron, talked to her about 45 minutes, and then I would catch the bus to work. We did not have cell phones, so at work I would call her on a pay phone that cost ten cents. After work, I hung out on the streets with my friend, and then made a bee line to Shar'Ron's house on 50th street where she lived with her family; Rev. Waco Sheppard, Mrs. Louise Sheppard, and sisters: Carol, Jo Ann (deceased), and Phyllis Sheppard, along with brothers: Lee, Freddie , and Glennn Dale (deceased). Also, there was the first born of them all; Marcellus who was killed in 1964 in the John Henry Brown school area and her four year old daughter, Valeicyia. Unknowing to us, God had a plan for us all.

Before I write about my then future in-laws, please allow me a moment to honor the memory of Margo Wilson. She was a very good friend to Shar'Ron and me for a long time, up to the time of her demise, She was a good hearted soul, funny, and was down to earth with everybody. She has a special place in my heart and I know that the feeling was mutual. Even until this day, we truly miss her.

Shar'Ron and Kenneth

Shar'Ron and I had a whirlwind courtship of two months. We were in love, real true love. I asked Shar'Ron to marry me. I had no job, and no place for us to live on our own. We applied for the license, took the blood test, went to the courthouse, and we were married. We told no one.

We went to my grandmother's first. We told her we married and we needed a place to stay. Shar'Ron was not at ease at my grandmother's. We then took the bus to her family. We would break the news to them next. We arrived at Shar'Ron's house, Momma-Dear Sheppard was in the kitchen cooking, we walked in the kitchen holding hands, and Shar'Ron announced, "Momma-dear, Kenneth and I are married and we need a place to stay."

Momma-dear was frying chicken, I remember so well she turned over a piece of chicken, grabbed the end of her apron , looked at us and said, "I will tell the boys, Lee & Freddie, both in high school to sleep in the den, and you and Kenneth can have their room."

I always wondered what the boys' reaction was when Momma-Dear gave them the news. The family has always treated me with love, even with the challenges I was destined to put them through. It was October, 1967, the beginning of times that would try the soul of this family and their cousins. I did not know it then, but God was directing my steps. Even in my sin, God was in control. God was directing everybody's steps. As I continue, you will see the Desperado who brought heartache and pain to everyone around him, me.

Teachable Moments

Redeemed by the Blood of Jesus

All in-laws are not in-laws from hell. Rev. Sheppard was a man of God and in spite of the chaos I caused in the family, he did not allow his disapproval of my actions to prevent him from allowing God to form his opinion of me and to embrace me with the love of God. I loved him for that.

Mrs. Louise Sheppard was a beautiful woman of God. She was not only my mother-in-law, she was also my spiritual mother and number one encourager. She knew me at my worse and yet gave me the best of her love. She was and will always be affectionately known as "Momma Dear."

Read and meditate on Prov.31:10-31, and Isaiah 40:13-14.

Always appreciate your in-laws, God connected you to them.

***

THE ROAD TO PERDITION

On Oct.30, 1967, Shar'Ron and I were married. We moved in with Shar'Ron's family in Oak Cliff. The middle room once occupied by Lee & Freddie was now ours and it felt like our own bridal suite.

Rev. Sheppard talked with me and made me feel welcomed. The girls made me feel right at home. The boys, well, I had to grow on them even though Glenn Dale and I went way back as friends — that's a story for another day.

I knew I had to get a job, and I did. I worked at a paper plant in Oak Cliff from three pm to eleven pm. I got to work without a problem, but I had to hustle to catch the bus downtown to take the bus to Oak Cliff. I did not want to ask anyone to come get me from work even though there were three cars at the house. Early November of the same year, I quit, I worked a few days with Rev. Sheppard at his part-time job for a week or two. Things were rolling right along smoothly right up to the Christmas Holidays.

One of Shar'Ron's cousins had a Christmas party at his house. I had not met any of her cousins, so at the party I found a corner, started drinking, minding my own business, but primed for trouble if it came my way. Boy did it come my way. Shar'Ron's cousin's wife asked Shar'Ron to ride to East Dallas to pick up another cousin and his girlfriend. Shar'Ron did not want to leave me at the party, so I went along for the ride. It was a cold December night, I was in the front passenger seat, and Shar'Ron sat between the driver and me. We picked up the cousins.

On the way back I cracked my window; the cousin ordered me to roll up my window using foul language. I answered him back with foul words, slipped my knife out of my pocket —turned in my seat on my knees, grabbed his shirt, pulled him to me, and stabbed him in his chest. Blood went everywhere—on me, on Shar'Ron, on the cousin's girlfriend. Everybody was hollering and screaming, the driver jammed her brakes, exited the car screaming, the cousin tried to exit the car but fell in the middle of Lancaster Rd. I jumped out of the car ready to take flight. Shar'Ron called out to me and we retreated to a phone in some nearby apartments. She called her brother, Freddie. There were no cell phones in 1967, so I had time to make my get away. It was about forty-five minutes before we were picked up.

When we got to Momma-dear's house, the phone was blowing up. The cousins at the party were calling and threatening me. Shar'Ron was on the phone, not begging on my behalf, but, letting them know, that I was a person to be reckoned with. Momma-Dear helped Shar'Ron and I move to an undisclosed location, not for our sakes, but for their sakes. They were driven by emotion, I was driven by the evil desire to steal, kill, and destroy by any means necessary. Dallas PD was looking for me; I got a job at the Lone Star School Book Depository, stayed off the streets, and partied at home.

> 10 The thief comes only to steal and kill and destroy; I have come that they may have life, (A) and have it to the full, (B)   John 10:10 NIV

In 1968, we moved on Fourth Ave. in East Dallas, and we continued to move again and again to various places throughout the year. We stayed close to her siblings, because they were loyal to each other. Even though they did not support my lifestyle, I experienced their loyalty firsthand. I worked at Lone Star a year or so, then we moved on Deer Path Ave. in Oak Cliff, and I got a restless itch. Shar'Ron was area jewel —putting up with me — defending me — scolding me and through it all she stayed. Inevitably, I found a side-chick.

I left Shar'Ron and moved with my grandmother to spend time with my side-chick uninterrupted. Shar'Ron was not working so she moved back to Momma-Dear's with Valeicyia. I took to the streets, courted a little while and in the summer of 1969, I was caught burglarizing a store in South Dallas, they already had a warrant for my arrest from the stabbing in December, '68; my fate was catching up with me.

I was sentenced to five years in Texas Department of Corrections for the assault to murder charge on Shar'Ron's cousin and the burglar case.

In June, 1969 I entered the Clemons Unit in Brazoria County to begin my sentence. I had been in the military prison, but Clemons was another world of work—death—and more work. From seven am to four pm we worked in the fields, running all day everywhere we went. They fed us good, but they ran it right out us. To underscore the treacherous prison system at that time, Clemons Unit was called the "Burning Hell", because of the heat and fast pace in the work fields.

Shar'Ron moved to an apartment on Grand Avenue with her cousin. She wrote to me and with the never ending support of her best-friend-forever, Margo, she decided to give me another chance. There was hope for us —despite my life of crime.

I was paroled in July of 1970. We left Huntsville at nine am and were scheduled to arrive in Dallas at one pm. Shar'Ron had a place for us, but instead of going home to my wife, I took a detour and went to Colonial Street in South Dallas.
There I saw all the old fellas, reveling in awe of me coming from the joint. They introduced me to a new wine Mad Dog 2020. I got drunk, started a fight (a few hours out of prison, on parole) about midnight, I staggered to where Shar'Ron was living.

When I arrived Margo let me in and told me Shar'Ron was in bed. I crept as softly as a staggering drunk could and decided I should just sleep it off because a staggering drunk and an angry woman were bound to be trouble. When I woke up it was so quiet I thought I was home alone, but the smell of bacon settled that. Shar'Ron gave me a dirty look as I came into the kitchen and the silence ceased when she dropped the plate she had prepared for me on the table. I knew she still had real true love for me because even angry she still fixed me something to eat. I got me a Job through the parole office working for the city cutting the grass at different sites in what they called the bull gang.

In 1971 Shar'Ron and I moved from Grand and the reckless life I had did not get better but worst. We were surviving on the $5.00 an hour I was making. Shar'Ron was the faithful wife, and I was the desperado husband, but she did not give up on me. I Was getting drunk every day at work and chasing skirt tails, thinking that I was a *player*. There are things that I did that will not be mentioned in this book to protect the memory of those that have passed on.
Shar'Ron's family probably did not like me much over the years back then, but they put up with me for Shar'Ron's sake. It made no difference to me, because I was always waiting for somebody to step out of line with me. That was the way it was back then with me. We had our ups and downs; Valeicyia was back and forth between being with us and staying with momma-dear. Around October of 1971, Shar'Ron and I separated and she moved to the West Dallas projects where her BFF Margo had moved. Well, I began to miss Shar'Ron and although I was staying with this lady in south Dallas, about the time December rolled around, I was ready to get back home. So, for the holidays, the city gave us a turkey, $100 bonus, plus our pay.

I called Shar'Ron over to Margo's house in the projects and begged her to allow me to come home.

She was young and beautiful, I knew that she had a male friend, but I could not argue that point considering my track record. I presented her an offer of everything that I would get from the city would be completely hers if she let me come home, and she said yes.

On the last day of my job for holidays, I got my turkey and my money, I was not going to the lady I was staying with, I was going to West Dallas where my wife was. I caught the bus to West Dallas to meet Shar'Ron over at Margo house and then we would go to Shar'Ron's house. I arrived, and greeted Margo, and her two children (Kenneth and LaTonya) and our daughter Valeicyia. We went home to Shar'Ron's little project apartment fixed up to the max.

Shar'Ron have always been a great house keeper and interior decorator I was high from drinking, and in the holiday spirit I had a turkey and $400.00 in cash, this would be a good Christmas (so I thought). I turned everything over to Shar'Ron and got ready to party with her.

Shar'Ron said she and Margo was going to catch the bus to the North Park shopping center. It was about one o'clock in the afternoon. Shar'Ron took Valeicyia down to Margo house where a friend was going to keep the kids. She said they would be back by six o'clock pm.

They left, and I sipped on wine at home and cut it up with the friends in West Dallas. These were friends that were big time dealers deep in the dope game I had known for years. About six pm, no Shar'Ron, (no worry), eight pm no Shar'Ron (getting hot under the collar) walked down to Margo, no word from Shar'Ron.

Time got later and later; I was drinking and walking the streets, mad because my mind was on one thing, that girl took my money and was out partying with another man. About five am, I took a hammer and busted up everything breakable in the house, T.V, glass coffee table, and mirrors. I took a knife and cut the bed linen, sofa, and chair. I wrecked the place, and then I went to Margo's and called Shar'Ron until she answered the phone. Finally, I told her what I had done.

About six am, Shar'Ron returned home with Glenn Dale, her brother. They did not know what to expect. I had pulled-up a chair in front of the door, and sat waiting for things to jump off. They came with a sense of calmness, no hollering and cussing. They knew if they set it off like that, there was going to be a blood bath. My blood or theirs; it made no difference to me. Violence was what I lived for. They talked a little trash, in a kind way being careful not to go too far.

Soon afterward, I just left Shar'Ron with her trashed-project-apartment. Shar'Ron moved on Goldman St., right off Bickers Avenue.

I knew the number one person in the drug culture in Dallas. I was hired as an enforcer; I moved in with family who welcomed me, my connections and criminal mentality. Their house was the hub of other crimes, not just me doing my job and an enforcer—watching dope I asserted myself in West Dallas and went full throttle gangster. I carried two guns and had a sawed off shotgun. We used dope, but didn't sell it. West Dallas was a city within a city and everything was connected to the criminal element. It was a dangerous place for a young ladylike Shar'Ron and my daughter Valeicyia to be. Shar'Ron and I talked. We decided I would move back in and protect her house from the druggies, robbers, and the criminal elements.

I went by Shar'Ron's house once a week to show my presence in her life and then I would go back to my posse. We were gambling, girls were tricking, and beating folk out of their money. We robbed, stole and used drugs. My reputation grew throughout Dallas. Shar'Ron's house was not bothered, neither was she or our daughter. My reputation protected them when I was not there. I also dropped money off at Shar'Ron's house once a week.

One day as we made our daily round, the boss man and a few of us were at a bar in Arlington Park. I was the look out in the parking lot. I was approached by two white boys who knew us to be the source of the "good dope". I told them to wait outside. I went to the man. He did not want to do business with them; I said I was going to burn them. The man said ok. He did not know what I was talking about, but he was letting me know he did not care what I did to them

We pulled up to the joint; they gave me the five hundred dollars. I left them in the car, because the people might think they were undercover police. I went in the cafe, asked where the back door was, and gave a person twenty dollars to take me to my hide-out house on Rupert in the projects. There, I laid low for three days while the white boys rode the projects looking for me. Nobody would tell them anything, but everybody kept me abreast of the white boys' every move.

One night I walked from Shar'Ron's on Goldman Street, to the other end of the projects to meet the posse. I was always had two guns on me. I was always vigilant, but that night I was on top of every car that passed me by when I saw a car with the lights turned off. As it came closer, I stepped quickly to hide behind a parked car. All of a sudden, their guns were blazing toward me, and I was hit in my right thigh. I fell to the ground. Shot in my leg, I pulled my two guns and fired at the dark silhouette of the car, emptying my guns. The car roared off into the dark and I dragged my right leg to my posse-house. When I arrived, I could not stand up. I lay on the on the front porch and banged on the door.

I was a bloody mess.

Everybody was there; my girl, her mom and her boyfriend, grown nieces (two) and their boyfriends, it was a houseful, and they were running around like chickens with their heads chopped off. I could not go to the hospital because I was wanted on a Federal warrant for firearm possession by a convicted felon.

I got them to get sheets, alcohol, wine, and drugs for pain. My niece's boyfriend worked at Texas Instruments. They put his insurance card in my pocket and called the ambulance. I went to the hospital under an assumed name. The doctor said if the bullet had been to the left one inch, it would have severed the main artery in my leg. I would have bled-out since I waited almost two hours before I went to the hospital. The bullet went clean through and they cleaned the wound and sent me home. The posse stayed with me and brought me to the house.

I did not get my prescriptions, as a result, my leg swelled. I did drugs, drank alcohol, and partied for about a month. My leg swelled so big, I had to cut my right pants leg off at the pockets to put my pants on. Everybody kept telling me that my leg was stinking. I did not notice because I stayed drugged all day. I became unresponsive and the posse became afraid. They put me in the back of the car, and drove me to Shar'Ron's house. When she opened the door, they explained to her my condition and they were bringing me home to die .Everybody, including Shar'Ron piled in the car and headed to the hospital. When I arrived, the emergency room doctor looked at my leg and paged two more doctors. I was in excruciating pain. The posse did not allow me any drugs because I was going to the hospital. Three doctors examined and smelled my leg. They concurred I had gangrene in my leg and in my system. They concluded they would have to amputate my leg.

I raised hell—to put it mildly. I said, "NO WAY!"

I was told if they did not amputate, I would die. I signed the papers giving consent to amputate. I went to surgery. When I woke up in the recovery room, the first thing I did was reach for my leg, and there it was! It was raised in a sling, opened with a slit on the inside of my right leg and a slit at the back of my thigh to allow the wound to drain. Lying in the hospital with my leg in a sling, and multiple streams of IV's, I did not have the sense to know it was the grace of God that diluted the gangrene in my body. My life and my leg were , even though I had signed the consent form to amputate.

I knew I could not stay too long in the hospital because they would soon come around to make financial arrangements. I bugged the doctor for two weeks to allow me to go home. After two weeks, I still was not cleared to go home. I called a good friend to come get me and bring clothes to me.

He came. I hopped out of the hospital back to Shar'Ron's house in the West Dallas projects to recuperate. I had twenty stitches on the inside of my right thigh, and on the back of my right thigh I had fifteen stitches. They had to slit my thigh, and had clamps on the inside and the back to allow my leg to drain the poison out of my leg. I rested for two weeks at Shar'Ron's, got restless and had the posse come get me, crutches and all. Back at the posse's house, I drank, did drugs, and oiled my guns in preparation to seek revenge on those who had shot me. But, I soon learned that they had disappeared.

Every now and then, I would go see Shar'Ron, after all she was my wife, and I did love her in a weird way. About six months later, on one of my visits when I would spend a night or two, we got into a violent argument in bed. I was angry and jumped up to dress and leave, she asked about the house money. I told her I was taking the house money and leaving. I grabbed my pistol from the top of the closet where I kept it out of reach from children who might come over. I was walking around in my underwear waving my gun in Shar'Ron's face, scaring her to death. I stood in Shar'Ron's face waving the gun, out of fear and desperation.

She knew I was drunk and full of drugs. She punched my gun hand upward and the gun flipped out of my hand into her hands. She saw it done in the old cowboy movies and she did it — one in a million chances that it would work— and it did. She had the gun and I was drug crazy. I kept walking upon her to shoot me. She was crying and was mad as hell, yet she backed out of the hallway, into the bathroom, and into the tub. Standing in the tub, she was crying and trembling, and I turned to get dress and leave — I had the money in my boot, I could come back and get my gun later.
I turned my back—heard a shot and my right leg went numb. The same leg I was shot in by those who I had beat out of their money. She shot me behind my right knee, and I fell down the stairs.

Shar'Ron called the police, and told them I was a wanted man. They congratulated her and I went to jail. I was wanted for the violation of the gun act—ex-cons cannot own or get arrested for having a firearm or shotgun. I was now headed for Federal Prison.

***
The Hand of God Is

In retrospect, I know God's hand was directing Shar'Ron's and my life. While being carried to the Dallas County Jail and as I awaited the federal trial, the hand of God prevailed. Shar'Ron was finished with me. She had made up her mind to move to California with her cousin and to start a new life with our daughter. Shar'Ron gave me enough h respect and came to visit me in the county jail to let me know about her plans. Of course I did not want to hear that. I begged and pleaded with her. She was determined to leave. When our on-screen visit came to a close; I screamed at her, and let her know a thing or two. Things I would dare not repeat. She walked away. I went to jail and was sentenced to five years in T.D.C. for assault to murder on Sha'Ron's cousin, with the burglary case added. . Shar'Ron went to California.

I entered the federal prison outside of Texarkana, Texas. I was mad at the world. I was mad at God. I was mad at Shar'Ron. I determined while in prison, I would have my way—day for day—not looking for parole. I entered prison in January of 1972. After a year in Texarkana, I was transferred to the Seagoville FCI, twenty-two miles from Dallas.

During the time I was in Texarkana, Shar'Ron wrote me a letter and I noticed the return address was her mother's address in Dallas. She had gone to church and had given her life to Jesus. She was saved.

While we were in West Dallas, we stayed with Shar'Ron's sister who was saved. She attended Evangelist Temple C.O.G.I.C. the late-great Superintendent Travis Cannon was the pastor, along with his wife, 1st Lady Mother Margaret Cannon. To show respect to her sister, we accompanied her to service. We were exposed to God and it was not in vain. God had a plan for the both of us. I was glad for her, but I was not ready for "religion". I still had some "chicks" waiting on me in West Dallas.

One Saturday night, with nothing to get into on the unit, a friend from St. Louis and I decided to check out a church service. The Evangelist was an ex convict from California. His life seemed similar to mine. That night in 1973, I was convicted by the Holy Spirit. I gave my life to Jesus Christ. I accepted Him as my Lord and Savior in federal prison. Shortly thereafter, unbeknown to me, I was moved to Seagoville in the winter of '73.

Shar'Ron agreed to visit me while I was in Seagoville; we decided to give our marriage another try—this time with Jesus. Shar'Ron came to visit with her sisters, Joe Ann and Phyllis, our daughter, Valeicyia, and Patricia, Shar'Ron's sister-in-law. It was to be a new beginning for us.

It was Christmas, 1974 and we were given a two week furlough from December 23rd to January 3rd. Shar'Ron's sister, Betty was going out of town and allowed us to stay at her house. We were still married, so it was cool. We enjoyed ourselves, made plans in Jesus, and l learned in April of '75, I was going to a halfway house for 90 days provided I got a job.

***
Freedom

In federal prison, all inmates were required to learn a trade before they could be considered for parole. I chose welding. I passed the welding course with flying colors. I made parole in February of 1974. I was sent to a federal halfway house, an old hotel on Gaston Avenue in Dallas which had been acquired by The U.S. Bureau of Prisons. I was glad to have Jesus in my heart. I witnessed to those who knew my reputation before prison. Shar'Ron lived with her mom and sisters in Oak Cliff. I got my very first welding job in South Dallas at the W.E. Grace Manufacturing Company, welding tractor parts for $5.00 an hour. I gave Shar'Ron three fourths of my check so we could get our own apartment once I was released from the halfway house.

On weekends, I was allowed to leave on Friday evenings at five and return to the hotel Sunday evening by four. Life was good, I had Jesus, my wife and daughter, and I had a bona fide skill. It was not all easy. I did not know then what I know now. I was young in the faith; there were things I could have done better. I learned that trials and tribulations are a part of the Christian's life. They serve a purpose and are ordained by God. I thank God for Shar'Ron, she was a godly wife. She was my rock. When I was tempted to revert back to my old ways, she stood steadfast with me through Jesus Christ reminding me He was my Lord.

I was young in the faith and although we went to church, there were times when our faith was tried but with the teachings from the church, our faith was anchored in Christ. Often times on Sunday, because the services could get long, we had to leave church to get me back to the halfway house on time. The Lord blessed Shar'Ron with a 1974 red Pontiac LeMans and we were
on our way in Jesus.

After I finished my time at the halfway house, we acquired our first apartment in Pleasant Grove at the Cherokee Apartments on Jim Miller Road. Valeicyia attended E.B. Comstock Elementary School. We were happy together as a family, not without ups and downs, yet happy in Jesus.

We attended Evangelist Temple C.O.G.I.C. Church. We had a great youth ministry at that time. The late Bro. M. C. Shelton was president and would call on me to testify about God's Grace. I had been to prison three times by the time I was thirty years old.

We would go to church early Sunday morning for Sunday school—go to a 3:00 pm service with our pastor. We returned to Evangelist Temple for 6:00 pm youth ministry, YPWW, and 7:00 pm night service. God really blessed our family, Shar'Ron, Valeicyia and me. He had a plan for us. I don't have the time nor space to name all the Saints who poured the love and grace of God into our lives. We humbly thank them all.

In 1975, the State Jurisdictional Evangelist, Dr. E. L. Battle and Bro. M.C. Shelton made it possible for Sister James (Shar'Ron) and I to be two of four delegates sent to the International Youth Congress in Memphis, Tenn. We were accompanied by Mother Daelene Davis, and I was on program four minutes to give my testimony. It was a wonderful experience.

In 1976, I expressed to Pastor Cannon God had called me to preach.

"Be faithful to Jesus, be faithful to the church," was all he said.

Shar'Ron and I were faithful to Jesus and to the church. We enjoyed life in Jesus.

I left W. E. Grace Manufacturing Company and worked at a plant where we made rock drilling bits. I was making $6.00 an hour. In 1975, that was pretty good for someone with my background. By1980, Elder Cannon was appointed Pastor of Mount Calvary C.O.G.I.C. Church. The deacon over the youth ministry at Mt. Calvary, Brother Henry Robinson, along with the sisters who aided him in the ministry asked Pastor Cannon could I go to Mt. Calvary to lead the youth ministry. Pastor Cannon consented and I was appointed Youth Evangelist Sunday School Teacher for the male youth.
We also met each Friday at six pm for the "Holy Ghost Rap Session", a mentorship program God gave me for young men in high school going through the challenges of young adulthood. Many of those young men became godly men— elders, missionaries, and superintendents.

I ran revivals throughout the city. Friday night was youth night, and we went to each church in the East Dallas District which was Supt. Cannon's District. By1982, God blessed me even more and I was doing revivals out of town. God was really good to my family.

Please take heed and allow what I experienced be a warning to you. I made big mistakes. The more God blessed me, the less I felt I needed to attend Sunday school, bible band, and other auxiliary programs. I made choices that were not of God and those choices drained the Spirit of God right out of me. I will not blame it on the devil, because although the devil did what he does today—tempts us to do evil or go against the grain of God—I made the choice to get off track.

We moved to Richardson, Texas in 1980 Valeicyia was in a car accident, both her legs were crushed. God healed her and her legs and today they are perfectly normal. We had been in Richardson about three years and found myself drinking on the weekends, going to church as a hypocrite and easing further and further back into the world. Shar'Ron and Valeicyia were yet faithful to God as I slid back into worldliness. I continued to work because I loved welding, but I also started using drugs again. I was drinking, using the nasal inhalers (taking the cotton out of the inhaler, soak the cotton in a little water, and inject the medicine into my arm.) I made up my mind to leave the church.

Shar'Ron let me know that she would not continue to be my wife with me living like that. I decided to part ways with Shar'Ron on a Friday night in October, 1983. I was to preach at the youth night service. As I sat in service, I saw Elder Cannon go to his office. I decided to give Elder Cannon pastoral respect and informed him of my decision to leave the Lord. I knocked on his door, and entered his office at 6:45 that Friday night. I sat before him and tol him of my fateful decision. He called Elder Adams and told him to direct the services.

Pastor Cannon told Brother Adams to take his wife home after the service. We prayed together. We wept together, Elder asked me if there was another church I wanted to go to. That really hurt my pastor, but my mind was made up to leave. We talked to about three am that Saturday morning.

We hugged. He got in his car and drove off.
I stood alone in the parking lot of the Mt. Calvary
 C. O G. I. C. Church, looked up into the dark sky and said, "God, I know that I am wrong. But, my heart is not feeling you now.

I will not bring reproach upon your name by preaching your word with an impure mind. If I go to hell, hypocrite will not be named among my sins. My life is in your hands."

When the sun came up, I went to Richardson and told my wife and daughter goodbye. I proceeded to South Dallas.

Teachable Moments

Redeemed by the Blood of Jesus

Before I go any further, I want to re-visit my Mother, Mrs Pearl James. She prohibited me from coming to her house to crash that is to be a dope-fiend-vagrant, eating up her food, and not helping out at her house. Well, I went off on my mom, that is want happens when one is controlled by an unclean spirit fueled by drugs. I stomped away from my mother's house in 1987 and did not speak to see my Mother until 2008. I was estranged from my Mother for twenty-one years.

When I was released, my Mother walked into our apartment, looked at me and said, "That is my son."

My mom started attending church with my wife and I at the Evangelist Temple, C.O.G.I.C. I preached one Sunday, and she accepted Jesus Christ as Lord of her life. I asked for her forgiveness and she forgave me. God allowed my mom to be with us three years serving Jesus together as a family. My sisters saw how God moved with my mom, and they too embraced me in the love of God. My lesson to you my friend is no matter how torn up your relationships may be, Jesus is a restorer of all relationships. Give Jesus a try. Read and meditate on Psalms 51:12.

Family Matters

Mrs. Pearl James (Sister Baby) my mother A strong woman who loved her children.

Evangelist James and wife Shar'Ron with Sister Baby at the Evangelist Temple COGIC banquet in 2009. I attended my first formal function after release from prison in 2008. Sister Baby was so happy for us to be together.

My Sisters:

Standing from left to right: Lee Marilyn (Tiny), Zoe', Kenneth M. James (Me), Shar'Ron (peeping from behind), and Barbara

Sister Baby is seated with grandchildren: Zachary on left, Tashara on right, and the top of Sierra's head.....

The Sheppard Family

Rev. Waco Sheppard

9/10/1918 – 7/14/1990

Mrs. Louise Sheppard, (Momma-Dear) Shar'Ron's mother, a Godly woman who had the ability to be as fierce as lion and as gentle as a lamb she loved her children and all who came to her. She is holding her great-great grandchildren – the twins, Logan and London at 6 mos. old.

Shar'Ron Sheppard James, far right, Joann Sheppard Rockwell, (1951- 2020) Carol Sheppard Hall, Phyllis Sheppard Griffin—Shar'Ron & sisters

The Sheppard's

Phylis, Shar'Ron, Joann, Carol—Lee, Glennn, Freddie.

Marcellus died early at age 20 and is not in picture but remains embedded in our hearts

The Prison Ministry Team:

Triena Dabney, Evangelist Kenneth M. James, Shar'Ron S. James,

Our Family — Grandson, Jarius with Logan (Great- grandson) on his back. Valeicyia, Daughter——London (Great-grandson)——Ebonee (Granddaughter)——Ta'Michael (Granddaughter)——Micah (Great-

Great-Grandson Jaden

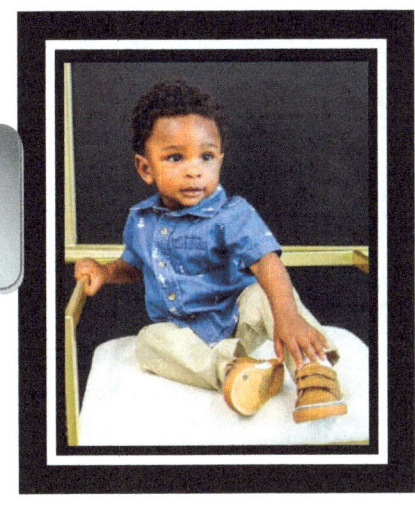

Granddaughter's Family
William & Ebonee Taylor
Wyatt & Everett

Shar'Ron & William

66

***
My Damascus Road Experience

I was welding at a shop on Lombardy Lane and had moved in with a girl and her family who received a check once a month. My weekly check was a welcome addition. After about two years with her, I quit my job and reconnected with those in the streets I knew before I gave my life to Christ in South, East, and West Dallas.

I began using drugs more frequently (cocaine, heroin, and rock cocaine), I was also selling and using "sets"— prescription combination drugs for seizures. I had no set dwelling place and became what we called a rolling stone— wherever I laid my head was my home. I raised so much hell wherever I went; I could not be pinned down to one place. I was well known everywhere in Dallas.

A young lady I did drugs with asked me to go to church with her. I told her no; because I made a deal with God—as long as I was doing my thing, I would not set foot in His holy house. She bargained in order for me to continue to have her, I must go to church. I went to church with her one Sunday. Without my knowledge, she told the Pastor I was a preacher. Well, after service, the sent for me and advised he heard I was a preacher. I told him I was a back-slider. He retorted there was no such thing and told me to be ready to preach the next Sunday. He would bring me before the church before I preached.

I shared this meeting with the young lady and decided I was not going back. That is until I found out I would receive two hundred dollars from the Pastor. This did not include what the members would give when they came up to shake my hand. All I could see was plenty of free money for dope.

The next Sunday, I went to the pulpit, went through the formalities, and rehearsed what I had spoken for years when I was in Christ. God was not in the message, nor was Heat that church. I collected almost $300, and spent I tall on dope.

The following Sunday, one of the choir members asked me out to dinner—I said ok—Monday I moved in with her. She had a good job, a home in Oak Cliff, and all she asked was for me to stay off the comer of Pine & Colonial.

Three months before I hooked up with the money-church, I had been busted for selling dope in Pleasant Grove. I was bailed out and I missed the court date. Now, my picture was in the wanted section of crime stoppers in the newspaper. There was a $5,000 reward for information about where I was.

I went into hiding; I bailed on the church, and the girl. I knew somebody would give me up and sure enough somebody did. I never found out whom. I was sentenced to eight years in state prison. The lady and the church stood by me on the promise I would come back to them upon my release.

I went back to prison again in 1988 for selling drugs. I knew that I would not be gone long. In the late eighties the prison population was so overcrowded, they were releasing prisoners fast like it was a revolving door. The state made a killing from processing inmates into prison—not by how long they stayed.

On June 26, 1990, I was released from prison with $200 of prison compensation. In the Texas prison system whether you did one year or one hundred years, all you got upon release was $200.

***

Freedom Again

I was consumed with violence, hate, and malice for all men and women. Why, because, I was possessed with evil. True is the Word of God.

> [43] When the unclean spirit is gone out of a man, he walketh through dry places, seeking rest, and findeth none. [44] Then he saith, I will return into my house from whence I came out; and when he is come, he findeth it empty, swept, and garnished. Matthew 43-44 KJV

As I walked through the gates in Huntsville, Texas to freedom again, I immediately purchased a fifth of Thunderbird wine, a pair of denim pants and a pair of L. A. Gear tennis shoes. I boarded the bus, settled down, and sipped my wine — eager to get to Dallas. I was not eager to greet my mother or any family member who might be at her house waiting for me. I was eager to smoke crack cocaine, get some girls and get back to making money, all in that order.

The Greyhound bus came through South Dallas on Lamar Street to the Greyhound bus station in downtown Dallas. After entering the Dallas city limits, the bus sped down to Lamar St. and as the bus approached Pine Street, I asked the bus Driver to let me off at Pine Street. The bus driver complied and allowed me and four others off the bus. I walked the two blocks from Lamar to Colonial Ave. Once on Pine Street, I was ready to let Dallas know that I was back. I forgot about the dinner my mom and my sisters prepared for my homecoming, I was a very selfish—you know what.

As soon as I stepped on the corner, people saw me and gathered around. I picked a girl, sent her for some "rocks", and went to the motel. Afterwards, I knew that it was time to go to work, not on some job, but doing what I did best, enforcer of the streets. I observe in the little time I was gone; a group of another ethnic persuasion had taken over my territory.

That did not set well with me. I did not like these people, they meant nothing to me, and to add salt to the wound, everybody on the corner of Pine and Colonial feared them. Oh, but I had a plan. I was going to bring these people down, if it kills me or I kill them—every one of them, the sisters too.

Somebody went to my mom's house and told my sister, Tiny. She came to the corner and we talked, I told her not to come looking for me again, and I was not going to report to parole. They would have to send me back to prison or I will die on the streets. I was a man with no hope whatsoever. Tiny left the corner crying.

I did not want these people to know my relatives because it was known; if they could not get you, they would hurt your kinfolks, male or female. I was going to wage my own private war on them. My rep was already established. I did not disclose to anyone what I was going to do, but I needed eyes and ears on the streets. I got a young lady who declared her loyalty to me. She was a crack-head and you knew how much you can trust a crack head, I know, because I was a crack-head (rock cocaine), I shot powdered cocaine and heroin in my arm.

The WAR

I did not have to do much to instigate my war on the people who took over my corner; they knew about me. They sent word to me that they wanted to talk. I went to their trap house (where drugs were sold) and they asked if I would work for them. This happened about four hours after I got off the bus from prison, June 26, 1990. I accepted on one condition, I wanted a pump shotgun and a pistol. They balked, but knowing that "jackers" (people who robbed dope houses) were plentiful and keeping in mind my reputation, they gave me what I asked for.

The next day I started working for them, my job was an enforcer. I made sure that nobody came to buy dope with weapons, made sure the one selling the dope did not steal or smoke dope on the job. We opened at ten in the morning and shut it down at ten at night. We were doing pretty good money wise. I was paid $500 cash every Friday, plus I got all the free dope I wanted. They were racking in $10,000 in a good week. Of course, I trusted no one. The girl with me was loyal only for fear of her life. My reputation had been solidified over the years everywhere in Dallas. My street name was *Unk* — short for uncle. Things flowed on point June—July—August—money was always on time, I had gained their trust. Remember, I had a plan from day one.

I suggested they up their dope volume from $10,000 to $15,000. They were reluctant at first, but eventually they came around to my way of thinking. Now, at the same time there was a big time drug dealer (whom I had known for years) was trying to get me to work for him, but I was on a mission of destruction. I met with him and let him in on my personal mission. He asked me not to do it. His objection was to no avail. However, he was my confidant and he let me know when it went down, I was welcomed to come and be with him. I consented to that.

September, 1990, was the target date for me to set things off. The second week of September we had $15,000 dollars worth of rock cocaine in the trap (house where drugs were sold). There were no cell phones back then, we used pagers. The procedure was—when we sold $500— I paged them—they came, picked up the money and left. They were scared of getting busted, which worked in my favour.

On the day I was going to declare war, I instructed my girl not to show up on the corner. She was to wait at my friend's trap. When the first $500 was made, I pocketed the money and did not page the people. I knew they were not coming on the corner unless I paged them. After the fourth $500 was made, I pocketed the money. I closed the trap down. The guy who was selling was looking like what the .... I walked up to him and asked, "Do you want to die?"

"No." his body trembled in fear. He knew something was about to go down.

"Put the dope and the money in a bag." I ordered.

He asked no questions and did what I said. He knew I would kill him if he didn't.

"Who do you fear me or them?" I knew my reputation was as strong as ever and he would not stand up to me.

"You Unk, I fear you." His eyes were wide with fear and uncertainty.

I hesitated for a moment, if I didn't kill him certainly the people would. But I had no beef with him. I gave him four fifty dollar rocks, two hundred dollars cash, and told him to disappear; he took what I gave him and flew the coop. I put my stash in a bag and left the empty trap and proceeded to my friend's trap, which was about six blocks from the corner.

When I arrived at my friend's trap, they were amazed I had the balls to pull it off. He assured me I had his soldiers behind me and I need not worry about them folks. I was not finished but it was time to party. About three hours later, the people knew what I had done. The corner knew what I had done and all hell broke loose. Dope fiends were coming to score dope at my friend's trap with warnings for me. The people were looking for me and there was a contract on my life.

It was on and I was ready. I had my pump shot gun, a 357 long barrel revolver, and hollow point bullets. They weren't coming to my friend's trap because he ran a family business of criminal activity. I was in a safe house but I was not going to hide out in my America, in my hood, in my city from a bunch of foreigners. When the time was right, about one in the morning, I got a two gallon can of gas, loaded my pup, my pistol and headed to my enemies' trap by way of back alleys. I crept up the alley until I was in the bushes across from their trap. I lay in the bushes and watched them go in and out of the trap. I knew the layout of the trap well; it was ours before it belonged to them.

After an hour or so, they all went upstairs (the trap was upstairs) and the bottom was empty. I waited about another hour to make sure movement was over.

Then, like a US Marine in battle, I crawled across to a bedroom window on the bottom floor. I climbed in and took my can of gasoline and poured the gas from the front to the back of the down stairs apartment. I backed out of the window and threw the gas can on the floor, took out my lighter, and ignited the room. As the room ignited in flames, I ran across the alley and waited in the bushes with my pistol. It didn't take long for the people to run down the stairs and I fired at them, forcing them back in the burning building. That was a rap.

They persisted on killing me; word on the street was they hired an assassin from New York to kill me, which marked the second contract on my life. This time, I did not sneak upon them. Against advice from my friends, I took the fight straight to them. I loaded my 357 magnum and proceeded to the corner. I did not know the face of the man hired to kill me, so I enlisted help of one of the girls on the corner. The reward was three rocks if she would point out the assassin to me when he rode upon the corner.

She let me know he always went to Poplar Street—parked—then walked through the alley. I paid the cocaine and told her to get lost. I located my spot—climbed the fence into a backyard—hid in the bushes, and waited for him to pass by. When he did, I jumped him from behind, and put that bi pistol under his chin with great discomfort. I took his gun and marched him out of the alley to Colonial Street and made him get on his knees facing me. I slapped him in his mouth with that big pistol—blood went everywhere.

I stuck my pistol in his mouth, and told all his people with their guns drawn on me if they didn't drop their guns, I would see them in hell. I was going to kill the assassin one or two of them.

By that time my some of my friends who had been in the bar next door heard Unk was at it again. They came out to back me with a show of force. I wanted to kill the person sent to kill me but the pleadings of my friends talked me out of it. Some of the soldiers wanted in on the action, so I let them have him. The people called a truce and left the corner. My friend had all of their customers back and my reputation went through the ceiling.

I made a lot of money during that time of criminal activity in my life. I treated everybody fair and not one person crossed me or stole from me. Years later, Shar'Ron told me someone who knew us both told her about the second contract and her response was, "I don't care, as long as he doesn't come around me."

That incident solidified South Dallas with drugs. My friend opened a trap house in Oak Cliff. He sent me there to enforce the law. I was with a girl, nobody special just someone to use at the time. She stole two rocks of cocaine from the bag, When my friend came to count up, the money did not add up. The bag was two rocks short. I know I didn't have them and the boy selling did not have them so that left only the girl. I asked her if she had them she said no. I asked a second time she said no again. I pulled out my gun and pointed it at her. I told her to strip. When she was naked, I gave her two options; leave and walk the streets naked or die. She chose life—I never saw her again. My friend got another trap house in South Dallas, and I traveled between the houses dispensing my brand of street justice as I saw necessary.
An incident occurred that sticks with me 'til this day. I was in a juke joint and a young lady came behind me to place an order at the bar. I stepped to the side to give her more room and I looked at her.

She dropped her beer and screamed, "look at his eyes—demon—demon." She ran out of the joint.

We all just stood around looking dumb founded. I never saw her again.

Another incident occurred at a motel. I went to the vending machine for cigarettes. Just before I walked away from the machine, I felt a tap on my shoulder.

"Do You Have a Light?" A voice said.

I turned to offer a light and the young lady looked at me and started running and shouting, "Demon eyes—demon eyes."

These incidents happened about a month apart. From that moment forward, I knew my soul was hell bound and I did not care.

Teachable Moments

Redeemed by the Blood of Jesus

The war covers another black part of my life as a criminal. It took place in a part of South Dallas known as "the corner". I have a son, Kenneth Smith. He was born three years before I married Shar'Ron. I was not a good father, nor a good role model. He was a young adult and saw all the things I did. I am not proud of what I portrayed to my son. But, my son and his mother are a part of my support system. He constantly tells me that he is not bitter about the past. He loves me.

This is God`s amazing grace. Listen, no mattered what has transpired, your life is in God`s hand and He will allow things to happen in your life on your road to redemption or in the case of believers, on your road to victory!

By the way, my son, his mother, and Shar'Ron and I have a good solid godly relationship. God is a restorer of all relationships when you trust Him as Lord of your life.

Read and meditate on 2 Corinthians 5:17-21 and Matthew 6:33.

***
Continuation

The drug houses in South Dallas, I went back to work in the south. The *jackers* were getting bolder and bolder in robbing the traps. We had two houses about four blocks apart in the south. I proceeded to make examples of those I suspected of trying to *jack us*. Things were getting so bad, I recall being at a carwash on Lamar Street, and I was given a tip about some young fools who were trying to rob the dope house. I rewarded the tipster with a rock—a solid cocaine the size of a dime coin which cost ten dollars. The tipster led me to where the culprits were gathered at the mouth of the alley behind the trap. I dismissed the tipster, and walked up to the culprits they knew me and my reputation. We exchanged pleasantries, and then I pulled out my big pistol, told them to raise their hands and walk down the alley. I directed them through the bushes where I proceeded to take their guns. The street code is you do not carry a weapon with you when you go to score dope. To do so, invites trouble with no questions asked. We were in the backyard of a vacant house, with over grown weeds and bushes everywhere. I marched them inside the house and ordered them to lie face down on the floor. They were pleading for their lives; they were about 18 years old—kids playing grownup games. I was going to kill all four of them; when I heard someone calling out to me.

"Unk, Unk," it was my girl coming down the alley.

I called out to her and she came to the vacant house. She saw the guys on the floor, and pleaded for their lives. Through her begging, yelling, and crying out through crocodile tears that they were somebody's sons; I did not kill them. I had my gun in my right hand; she was holding my left arm, pleading for them. I told the young fools to get up and get out, with the promise that if I ever see them anywhere in South Dallas, I will shoot them on sight. They flew out of the vacant house, and no, I did not see them again— except for one. I saw one of them when I was later being processed into prison in Huntsville.

Word spread of what had transpired in the vacant house, my friend and I made money, money, and mo money. To keep allies on my side, I paid bills for girls who needed help, I gave dope to those who had no money, and wine to the alcoholics. Allow me to digress a bit; I was making $500 dollars a week. With all the dope I wanted for free. However, I lived a life of solitude. I didn't allow anyone to know where I slept at night. Most of the time it was in abandoned houses. I knew my time was limited. I did not waste my money on apartments, cars, or anything like that. I was a maverick, a tumbling tumble weed.

It was the winter of 1990. I was using drugs in my arms. I was smoking the rock cocaine. My daily diet was Thunderbird or Night Train (wines). The dope was morning, noon, and night. Every now and then, God would speak to me and I felt the urge to turn back to Jesus. I was a backslider—person who lived a Christian lifestyle and was no longer practicing the faith. The escapades of my lifestyle would not let me go. Two incidents come to mind:

First, I stood outside the cafe shooting the breeze with some of the guys. A church van rolled up in front of us, stopped and some teens got out. The guys standing there with me walked away cussing.

A couple walked up to me and asked if I knew Jesus as my Lord. I said no, but had to add I was a backslider. They prayed for me and two weeks later, I was in the bootleg house on Colonial Street loaded on drugs and alcohol.

Secondly, I was in one of my usual spots one evening at table with two others, and a girl sitting on my lap. All of a sudden, I felt a peace like I had not experienced in a long time. The tears began to flow down my cheeks, and the young lady exclaimed," that dope sure must be good". I just got up, walked outside stood on the curb and wept. Nobody said anything, they just looked. I knew what was happening; it was the grace of God. You see, when God is ready to reach you, it does not matter where you are, or what you are doing, He is able to reach you. As I write, I realize it was God who spared my life. At the time, I thought it was me sustaining my life. I thought I was invincible. I was living my version of *The God Father* movie. My life had spun out of control.

There was the time that the people I had the drug war with, earlier before the big conflict had kidnapped me off the corner and took me to the woods, put me on my knees, and put a pistol behind my head to kill me.

"I am not going to kill you Unk, because you look like my father back home." The gunman said.

They busted me up pretty bad, but they did not kill me. There was yet another time when I was with six others in a vacant house shooting dope into our arms, using one cup of water and one needle—mine. The seven of us used the same needle, the same water, shooting each other's blood into our veins. They are all dead now.

I was living life on the edge. Once a fellow owed me money for dope; I walked upon him partying and splurging money at the boot leg house, I sent someone to lure him outside, and when he came, I shot him. Nobody snitched, because they knew better.

I walked in the bootleg house, about 2:00 am during the Christmas holidays, a young lady came up and started hugging me, and whispered in my ear," don't look now Unk, but, there are two men here talking about killing you".

Well, I played along, hugged her back, and we acted like lovers, but in reality she was pointing out the two men sent to kill me. They were standing at the juke box watching me; I paid them no attention (so they thought). As the young lady and I drank Thunderbird wine, the two men turned their backs to play a record. I knew I had to act fast—no shooting— might hit an innocent person. I pulled my knife, and tipped up behind them. The first fella turned and I grabbed his head and with an upward thrust of my knife, I hit him in his heart— dead instantly. I pulled my knife out of him and blood was everywhere. His partner raised a beer bottle to hit me; I stabbed him in his stomach. The three of us slipped on the bloody floor. A friend of mine helped me up, pointed me toward the door and pushed me saying, "Run Unk, run."

***
The Road to Redemption

I ran from the bootleg house, slipping and sliding on the bloody-wood floor. It was mighty cold that night, thirty degrees. The belting sounds of sirens from the police and paramedics propelled me as I ran to my son's house, Kenneth Smith, aka Lil Ken and/or Sweetie. By the time I reached Lil Ken, the blood had coagulated on me. I knocked on his door and when he opened it, he thought it was me bleeding—I quickly explained what happened. I was two blocks away from the scene.

My son gave me a change of clothes and I sent him to the bootleg house to see what was going on and who was saying what. I in turn focused on a hot bath to wash my bloodstained body. Two hours later, Lil Ken returned; most of witnesses gave the police my name as *Unk*. But, one girl, whom I considered a friend, gave my real name. With that info, I knew they would put an APB (all-points bulletin) out on me; I already had a warrant for my arrest for parole violation. I was as hot as a fire cracker on the 4th of July and right then I swore to kill the young lady before I went back to prison—possibly for life.

I had a lot of rounds to make before the sun came up. I planned to hang out in West Dallas during the day, and at night I would sneak back to the corner to kill that snitch. Soon, the crime was all over the news on T.V. and on the streets. In West Dallas, I would hang out at the trap of those I knew. It was cold, and I needed money for wine and dope. The police were looking at all the places where I had hung out. Little did I know, people on the corner were pouring their hearts out to detectives downtown—some truth—some lies. Were they trying to get me the death penalty?

While I was on the run, I was given three murder cases. On their affidavits, I was considered armed and dangerous, shoot to kill on sight.

When the word got out on the streets, I was treated like a leper. I did not take it personal—that was street life, it was a matter of survival. They gave me money and dope, to get me away from them without me getting angry. At night I made my way back to Southside, waited in a vacant, cold house for the girl who gave the police my name. The hatred I felt for her was so deep, I vowed if I went to prison and ever got out, I was still going to kill her. If she died and I got out, I was going to dig up her body and cut her head off. I waited and watched for a month in the cold. Then, I went to the corner in the daytime, letting everybody know what my intention was.

I made it known; those who put their mouth on me were doomed. The girl hid out pretty good. I decided to just do what I do until I was arrested. I hung out boldly and openly on the Southside of Dallas. I did not concern myself with the possible haters because I knew I was still gravely feared in the hood. One day, word came to me that someone called the police. I slipped away back to West Dallas. I was in and out of Aunt Helen's house. She always welcomed me. I did not stay long because of the APB.

It became too hot for me to show my face in South Dallas, so I hung out in West Dallas where I continued the gravitas behavior that had me on the run. The people were bothered by police as their investigation made way to West Dallas. They were trying to flush me out. I was now a lone wolf—constantly looking over my shoulders—trusting no one. With nothing to lose, I took dope from the dealers and dared them to do something about it. I blended in with the homeless and walked pass many detectives. It was bitter cold every day, and my only warmth came from the fire barrel. The fire barrel was a fifty gallon barrel located on a corner or vacant lot. It burned wood, paper, and provided warmth to the homeless.

In a strange way, I knew the law was closing in on me. I had no money. I was cold, hungry, and alone. I needed dope and wine. I had nowhere to go because I was too hot—everyone stayed clear.

At one of my lowest points in December of 1990, I was cold, alone, and hungry.
I went to a Kentucky Fried Chicken restaurant in West Dallas. I hollered through the door and asked for the food they were throwing away. I walked a few yards from the door to give assurance I meant no harm. I was just hungry. Soon afterwards, food was put outside the dumpster, the worker waved at me; I retrieved the package and headed for the shelter. It was thirty degrees with a wind chill factor of seventeen degrees, and snow was piling up fast. The West Dallas projects were being demolished there were no doors and windows were open—hardly shelter. I sat on the bleachers in front of the vacant projects on Hampton Road trying to eat the chicken and fries left at the dumpster. A police car stopped in front of me with lights shining on me. I just knew I was going to jail—the car drove off without me.

After eating, I trudged through the snow and entered one of the vacant project units. The open doors and windows were conduits for the wind seemingly giving it more force. It was bitter cold, I curled into a ball, and listened to the howling wind. I reflected on my life and felt I was at ground zero. I had no family, no wife, and no friend, I had however, gained a whole lot of enemies. I remembered another young man in a similar situation—the prodigal son. I knew truth but I chose to believe the lies. On that could bitter night, I got on my knees and asked Jesus to forgive me of my sins. He did.

I was a 126 pound alcoholic on drugs who was tired of being sick and tired. At mornings first light, I emerged from those projects with no money, not even bus fare. But I knew God was giving me another chance, even though it would be in prison. I was alienated from every one. Shar'Ron divorced me in 1986. My mother and sisters loved me still and lived in fear of receiving that inevitable phone call to hear I was dead. I had nobody but Jesus, so together we walked down Singleton Avenue, over the Singleton Bridge to the Commerce Street Bridge to Lew Sterrett Justice Center.

***
The Road to Restoration

In order to fully appreciate the path of my soul's restoration, I must show the depth of my decent. I fell hard and deep into a life of pure evilness; life from which many have no return. In so doing, I give credence to those who loved me in spite of.

A noteworthy incident happened in 1978. Shar'Ron, Valeicyia, and I moved on Illinois Avenue in the Oak Cliff section of Dallas. We were attending church; I was a young minister and a hypocrite—sometimes in church, more times in the world. Shar'Ron and Valeicyia were yet trying to be faithful, despite my antics. I was working as a welder in West Dallas. One Friday evening, I went to South Dallas, got drunk and did not go home until Sunday afternoon.

I was ready for war when I reached the house. What I did not know was Shar'Ron had anticipated trouble and she borrowed her mother's pistol. When I entered the door she was standing in the hallway in front of our bedroom. We argued, I grew tired and pulled out a hammer. I sat in a chair in the front room facing her and stood up with the hammer in my hand. She emerged from the bedroom pointing a pistol at me. I sat back down real quick and before I could say anything, she shot at me. The bullet hit the left wing of the chair six inches from my face, I jumped up, and Shar'Ron fired again hitting me just below my left knee. I opened the door and she fired again hitting the door jamb. I hopped down the stairs and when I tried to run, my leg snapped where I had been shot. I fell to the ground and laid there until the police came. Shar'Ron stood over me, pointing the pistol at me—I thought she was going to kill me. Her sisters, Carol and Joe Ann, took the pistol from her and left with it.

I did not press charges, nor did I blame her. She did not go to jail. She filled out a police report and that was that. She moved, I stayed in the hospital, and went to Momma's house when I was released. My leg was in bad shape. I needed a place where I could be still.

My mother, Miss Pearl James, was a wonderful mother who gave me three sisters, Barbara, Zoe and Le Marilyn (Tiny). I was the eldest. They loved me. It hurt them to see me live the way I did. Momma gave her best for us and yet, I did not appreciate her. In the early eighties, Tiny was living with Momma and working as well. As for me, I was in and out of Momma's house. I went there to rest, and eat— only to leave until the next time.

The year was 1987. It was two o'clock in the morning and I staggered to my Momma's house to crash. She would not open the door; she told me I was not welcomed there anymore. I fussed and cussed sparing no explicative, and left on this note, "as far as I am concerned you have no son and I have no mother." I did not see my mother again until 2008.

***

In 1990, I sat in county jail, looking at a life sentence. I was in the old county jail. At forty-six, I was the oldest on the cell block which we referred to as the tank, with youngsters. I had the worst charge—first degree murder.

God was moving on my behalf. I took refuge in knowing I gave my life to Jesus in the vacant project. I obeyed God when He told me to turn myself in.

Satan would not have told me to do that. Satan would have kept me on the streets sinking deeper and deeper onto death. It was God who had begun a good work in my life and though a lot was left to be done, I was ready to turn to God.

In the tank there was a young man whose mother went to the same church I once attended, Mount Calvary COGIC. His mother brought him to a revival I ran at the church.

He was not a regular visitor, but he remembered them move of God that took place when he did come. He was glad to see me and told everyone in the tank I was a good man—despite the fact I was in jail.

When I was on the streets, living in sin, God sent an angel to me in the person of Sister Daelene Davis. She traveled the road of perdition with me constantly reminding me that God was not through with me. Her prayers, support, and encouragement in Christ were now coming into fruition. I went to jail with no money, but God touched the heart of those young men and they bought all I needed from the commissary. God used me to speak to the young men and they listened. The young man who recognized me asked me to tell some of the sermons he heard me preach. God was mighty in that tank as He used me to speak to the young men. They were all doing short time; I let them know that there was still hope for them and their families, wives, children, and parents. I encouraged them to attend chapel services and to consider giving their hearts to Christ.

In January, 1991, I went to court and was sentenced to thirty years in prison. The thirty year sentence was classified as aggravated, which meant I would not be eligible for parole until I had done fifteen years. In March, 1991, I was sent to TDCJ, with a thirty year aggravated sentence.

During that time TDCJ was in the manufacturing business. Because I was an experienced welder, I was sent back to the unit I paroled from in June, 1990. When I got off the bus, I was welcomed back by officers and inmates alike. My first question was, "when is Bible Study?"

I was determined to live for Jesus in prison or out of prison. I had to learn to make godly choices in a place that was 98% evil. But 2% of Jesus is greater than 98% of evil. My Road to Restoration with Jesus had begun.

Chaplain Fleming loved the Lord and he loved those in prison. I started the discipleship tract with the Survival Kit, a Bible study for new Christians. Church was the last thing on an inmate's mind we averaged thirty to thirty-five men in a Sunday service. I went to every ministry that came to us.

In prison you have to get permission to do any and every thing. We asked for permission to have prayer before starting work in the mornings, it was granted under the condition that I would be the only one to pray. I worked in metal fabrication, where I welded whatever was on the list. Every morning we prayed and all were welcomed to join in. I asked the Lord to bless our Morning Prayer knowing that if anything went wrong it would be on me.

The knock on Christianity in prison is that it is used to make parole. That was true then and stands true today. Many get saved and walk in the Faith while they are on the inside. As soon as they are released, they forget all about Christianity. I did not have time to worry about that. I had to deal with myself.

I started attending the Master Life Bible study facilitated by some brothers from Tyler, Texas including Brother Todd. We met every Wednesday night from 7 – 9 pm. One night the lesson was on forgiveness. The Lord convicted me for still harboring hate toward the girl who gave the police my name. I stood up and told the story. I asked the class and the volunteers to pray for me.

Brother Todd instructed me to reach out to all I could by letter and ask forgiveness for my words and actions toward them, including the young lady I was mad with. God was teaching me, and I was a willing student of the Word. I did as instructed and wrote the letters. Although I never heard from them, I did what God wanted me to do. In the act of obedience alone, I found peace, freedom and forgiveness.

I debated with inmates who were not saved and those who practiced other religions. God showed me I did not have to defend His name—just keep myself pure. That was hard to do in prison where no religion is respected, and the principal of faith is often misunderstood. For instance, I did not engage in anything that was against the rules of the unit, like gambling.

They gamble on everything in prison, especially sports. When they asked me to buy a square on a gambling board, I told them I was a Christian; they would laugh and tell me brother so and so is a Christian too and he bought a square.
Over the years, I learned as a Christian, my actions spoke volumes in prison.

The first three years in with Christ were the hardest. God peeled the world off me and pulled the world out of me by His Word.

I burned my eyes welding, and was moved to the kitchen where I let my guard down. I had no one to write or send me money. While working in the kitchen, I learned to steal meat and sell it to the inmates in exchange for what I wanted out of the commissary. It didn't take long for God to intervene and shut that down. While selling meat, I continued my bible studies and was up to number seven on the nine tier discipleship tract, when I was approached by Brother Darnell McCullough.

"You don't have to sell food, make a list and I'll get whatever you want." He said. I stopped selling food right then—that was God. Darnell stayed on the unit for the next 15 years and kept his word to me. Look at Jesus.

All inmates were tested for hepatitis in 1993. They discovered my liver enzymes were out of whack. I was sent to the prison hospital for a liver biopsy. My liver was wasting away. I was diagnosed with cirrhosis of the liver, stage one. My body had been severely damaged from living the street life; I was told I probably would die before I went home.

Although my blood enzymes were being monitored regularly, the truth is there is no top notch medical treatment in prison for anyone. After the doctor gave me the grave news; I remembered a Kenneth Copeland teaching from St. Matthew 8:16-18. I went to my bunk, opened my bible to the scripture in St Matthew, and prayed. I read God's word back to Him. I declared what I believed: Jesus not only bore my sins on the cross, but He also bore the disease that was in my body. I believed I was healed and decreed it to be so in the name of Jesus. I thought— what if he did not heal me. In resolve, I asked God to let His son, Jesus, be manifested in my life so that the inmates and officers would know Jesus as their Lord. After that prayer, I went on living for Jesus.

Every two weeks on Saturday, I went to the infirmary for my blood enzyme report. One Saturday, I walked in the infirmary, and sat across the desk from the nurse. She looked at my report and she looked: at me—she looked at my report, and she looked at me—she sat back in her chair shaking her head from side to side in unbelief. She declared that my liver enzymes were perfect and healthy. I gave God the praise right in the office as I testified of the goodness of Jesus!

I testified in the halls—in the chow hall—at work in the laundry, and on the recreation yard. I gave Jesus the glory! This was just the beginning. He would show up in a mighty way on the unit.

It was 1996; God had increased our Sunday church service from thirty to eighty men strong. More men were signing up for bible study. God gets the glory.

As I stated earlier, I attended the Chaplain's Bible study on the book of Ephesians. During a class, Chaplain Fleming (Chap) paused in his teaching and asked me a question before the class of twenty men. He asked, if cleared with the warden, would I carry the service and preach per his program for two weeks? He had to go to California for National Guard duty. Now at that time, this was unheard of in prison, and this was God, who specializes in the unexpected.

Chap cleared it, with the Lieutenant in the service to make sure everything was done in order. On the day before Chap left for California, he advised me and he prayed for me before he left.

That Sunday, the Lord blessed us mightily. The Lieutenant gave a favorable report to the warden.

I was growing in Christ, but it would not be long before I made a grave mistake. Before the next Sunday, I was pressured by this brother to let him preach the last service before the chaplain returned. I knew Chaplain Fleming left me in charge and I allowed the brother to preach. Everything went well, but Chap was not pleased with me because he left the service in my hands. We were in prison, not in the free world. I was learning—God was with me.

Chaplain Fleming was later diagnosed with cancer. He was replaced by Chaplain Rose of the Catholic faith. We prayed fervently for Chap. He would come in every now and again while taking chemo treatments. I will never forget the Sunday morning I entered the gym and noticed the sad faces and tears of the men. Chaplain Rose pulled me aside and gave me the news that Chaplain Fleming had passed on. He thought we should have a service but with him being Catholic, he thought it wiser for me to conduct the service.

I asked God for strength and wisdom to comfort the men's hearts. To this day I cannot remember what I preached, but God was in control. I was about five years into my sentence. Chaplain Rose worked overtime to accommodate our Bible studies since we did not have protestant chaplain. God bless him wherever he is.

We were without a chaplain; we served God as best we could in prison. Volunteers came in and helped with our services. The chaplaincy remained vacant. Royce Hall, Michael White, Willis Allred and others rallied around the men on the unit covering us all in prayer. Thank God for the bible studies, this enabled us to encourage each other. Royce Hall joined the Lover's Lane United Methodist Church pastured by Rev. Stan Copeland. He had plans for the unit. He was waiting o a chaplain to be assigned or hired. God had a ram in the bush— a volunteer, William Snidow. He had just been reassigned as Pastor of a Baptist Church in Palestine, Texas. He started with Promise Keepers, a group of men who visited various prison units in Texas to encourage the men. If memory serves me right, Chaplain Snidow in 1999 became a volunteer chaplain and therefore was able to apply for the chaplain job. Other applicants came through the unit, but none stayed.

Chaplain Snidow was God's man of the times. In 2000, William Snidow was hired as the Chaplain of the unit. The LLUMC would hold a symposium with twenty Christian brothers selected by Chaplains Snidow and Rose, to discuss the ministry of the Lord Jesus Christ on the unit through Alpha, a Biblical small-group bible study. I was one of the twenty selected along with Royce, Michael, Jerry Haga, Rickey Jackson, John Garcia and others in 2002.
The power of God's Holy Spirit in everyday living was what God used to grow His church on the unit. God used Chaplains Snidow and Rose to organize The New Testament Church of the Powledge Unit. Personally, I was in God's school.

I had been in touch with Shar'Ron. She had come with a ministry on occasion and ascertained she came out of kindness in Christ and I should not read anymore into it. Six months past before I heard from her again and I heard she was getting married. Evidently, God had a plan for us that we did not know.

In May 1998, I received a letter from Shar'Ron. I was surprised, because I thought she was married. When they called my name at mail call, I immediately looked at the return address. It was her mother's address on 50th street in Dallas. I went to my bunk, opened the letter, and read:

Dear Kenneth,
If you are standing up—sit down.
God spoke to me and told me to take you back as my husband. Naturally,
I wrestled with God, but God prevailed.

We started on a ten year journey—me in prison—her in the free world.

I would like to acknowledge Mother Darlene Davis, for her ministry, dedication to the lost, and her commitment to Jesus Christ. She played a key role in my deliverance an d in the making of me, a man redeemed by God's amazing Grace.
Until we meet again, Mother D.

***
Inside Restoration

Throughout the eighteen years I spent in prison, God was shaping me according to His will by trial and tribulations.

Chaplain Snidow was appointed by God to the vacant Chaplain position. In 2001, Chaplain Snidow shared a vision he had with me. He told me God had a purpose for my life for His glory. The hand of God began moving in my life with the organization of the New Testament Church of the Powledge Unit.

Chaplains Snidow and Rose spoke with the officers and inmates on the unit, at the next Sunday service they stated the vision to the congregation. They called Ricky Jackson, Jerry Haga, and me to the front of the church. We were not aware of what was going on. Chaplain Snidow asked the church to approve of us becoming the first Elders of the New Testament Church of the Powledge Unit.

The church accepted us, and later on we were ordained. The chaplain, deacons, choir, and the order of service were adopted. Chaplain Snidow had us in training in all aspects of church servitude and church leadership. The volunteer staff was cut in half.

God had me in transformation mode. My flesh was being transformed. First, Captain Franklin, head of laundry, promoted me to laundry dispenser. This meant the bleach was taken out of the hands of the laundry washmen and I alone had the key to the bleach—I dispensed the bleach in the washer.

The washmen were stealing and selling the bleach and no clothes were getting bleached. Bleach was like gold in prison. One could wash in their cells; have white socks, and underwear, along with commissary-bought shorts, and other items. When word got out on the unit, the inmates approached me to steal and sell bleach to them. I lived the best I could for Jesus before these men, and yet they tried to influence me to steal by offering me commissary goods such as coffee, soap, toothpaste, food, and other things. Captain Franklin gave me that job at the advice of Chaplain Snidow. Thankfully, I had a good prayer partner and brother, Royce Hall. He always stood for Jesus. We encouraged each other.

No one believed a person could live a clean and obedient life for Jesus. I was threatened, talked about, and cursed for not stealing. It was widely believed we were running game to make parole. I was the job for about 5 years, every day I was in spiritual conflict with the evil in others. Once, l told God I was tired of all the trouble, and I was going to quit. But, God put a stop to that way of thinking. I was growing in grace and God reassured me that He was with me. I was to trust Him alone. The temptation to lash back was there, but, my faith in Christ was greater and I was victorious in God. Sure there were moments when I was afraid, and I learned the weapons-of our warfare are not carnal, but mighty through God—2 Corinthians 10:4.

There are many gangs and religions in prison other than Christianity. One group in particular always recruits the blacks for their movement. This movement was, is, and always will be in conflict with Christianity. I was called to speak at their black history program. I asked who did they want me to speak about and I was told to speak on anyone of my choice. I prayed, and God told me to speak on Jesus. With this group, that was a no, no. They knew that I was a Christian, but God worked it out for me to be a witness in the enemy's camp.

The day came for the program; I went to the meeting alone (except for Jesus in spirit). I sat in the meeting as they went through their rituals, before the speaking started. The first person spoke about the founder of their movement. The second spoke on Malcolm X. The third spoke on Martin Luther King. I spoke for ten minutes about Jesus Christ. I spoke for ten minutes about Jesus Christ, the Son of God. When I finished, the room was silent—you could hear a pin drop. The silence was cold, still and felt like death.

The free-world-volunteer for their religion stood up and ordered the sergeant at arms to escort me out of their meeting. I was despised by the inmates who supported that religion. They cursed me, threatened me for desecrating their service. I wanted to strike back. My homeboys wanted to back me up. I was compelled by the Spirit of God to hold my peace. Though it was not easy to do, I obeyed God.

Some of the group's members saw the Christ in me and enquired about my faith. I shared Jesus with them and one of them decided to give his life to Christ. That is when the enemy struck. One morning as we filed into line to for breakfast, suddenly, I felt a blow to the back of my head, my glasses flew off my head, and I felt an explosion. While I was looking for my glasses, the fella who caught me by surprise and hit me from behind grabbed me by my belt and by the collar of my shirt. He was 6'6" and at least 360lbs. He attempted to body slam me on the concrete floor. As he tried to raise me, I grabbed both of his ears. He could not raise me because I had his ears and every time he tried to raise me I pulled on his ears. His pain was harsh. The correctional officers were there in three minutes, broke us up and hand cuffed us. God was in control. He was teaching me a lesson of faith. The lesson was: no matter how unfair life seems, no matter what tragedy happened, God was in complete control and He gives us an opportunity for victory. We went to court, were given 15 days in seg (segregation) or solitary confinement. God was up to something. I did not know what—I knew He was in control. I was in my twelfth year of confinement, God was still transforming me. Even in what seemed like a bad situation, God was bringing glory to Himself. They allowed me to have my Bible, I prayed to God for wisdom and strength.

In seg you are in a cell alone, but you can talk to other inmates in other cells by calling out. I was defending myself, but fighting was an automatic five year set off when your parole hearing came up. About that time, I was due for a parole hearing. I had no option but to trust God, which was not easy. But, God helped me. Knowing and trusting that God is in control has served me well even after I was home on parole for thirteen year

While I was in seg, I received two unexpected visits, one from the Warden and the other from the Major. They basically came to enquire what happened. I did not know that the light of Jesus Christ was shining all the way to the front at the administration building. They understood I did not start the fight and was defending myself. It was so noted in my files which helped me when I was up for parole again. That was the move of God—the Warden and Major cared for no inmates. A day or two later, the Holy Spirit told me to apologize to the big guy who ambushed me in the hall. I resisted, but God had me in the school of love your enemies. I obeyed the Lord, and apologized. I also let him know that contrary to popular opinion circulating on the unit .I was not going to retaliate on him. I let him know it did not matter what he or anybody else thought about me, I was a Christian and will remain a Christian.

When our days were up in seg, my-home-boys who remembered my old reputation kept talking retaliation, which I quickly put to rest. The fella who hit me was calling me a coward—on the streets I was bad with a knife—but in prison I was a coward. I held my peace—endured the harassment as a good soldier of Jesus Chris. This was not easy because I knew I feared no man, in prison or not.
I thought I had lost my job as the bleach keeper in the laundry, but the captain of the laundry wanted me back. I was re-assigned to the laundry.

God allowed trials of all kinds to visit the brothers on the unit who were giving their all to Jesus, to build our faith and to make us complete in Him. God was with us. We had a purpose. Our purpose was to allow the Lord to be glorified in our lives so that the men on the unit could see Jesus.
The church was being formed.

Chaplain Snidow and the three elders picked deacons, and a worship leader. The chaplain had the elders in a homiletics class to properly train us for service in the Lord. The chaplain allowed us to carry the service twice a month and volunteers came in twice a month. Back then, we had service on Sunday mornings at 9am to 11am.

God was blessing Shar'Ron and I. She came to see me often. She would bring the grandchildren, Ebonee, Ta'Michael, and Jarius. They were pretty young, but I enjoyed them when they came.
The Lover's Lane United Methodist Church started the Alpha Smart Group Bible study on Wednesday night. The group helped many men to grow in grace and in the knowledge of Jesus Christ. I came up for parole five times and was denied five times with a 2-yearset off each time.

When I finally made parole it was with the stipulation I would go to an eighteen month reentry program, Inner Change Freedom Initiative in Houston, Texas for eighteen months. Though I was not happy with that, I was willing to allow the will of the Lord to be done with my life no matter how I felt about it.

***
The Final Test Before Home

Before I tell you about God's finishing touch in my life during-the 18 months in Interchange Freedom Program, I want to go back to my original unit where God began His plan of purging ,restoring and transforming my soul to a lifestyle of holiness. Remember, because I lived apart from God for so long and hard, He had to peel back layers and layers of flesh from me.

> "Brethren, if a man be overtaken in a fault, ye which are spiritual, restore such an one in the spirit of meekness; considering thyself, lest thou also be tempted."
>
> Galatians 6:1 KJV

This is a key scripture for all to learn and know. The key word is overtaken, which means ambushed, surprised, or overwhelmed. When a Christian is overtaken by sin, he is acting without thinking and is not sinning willfully. When overtaken, a Christian will immediately repent to God and to those he has offended—one of my many valuable lessons learned during my time in the reentry program. I remain grateful to Chaplain Snidow for recommending me to this faith-based program.

During imprisonment my soul, faith, and sanity were tried in many situations. Take prison lockdown for instance, which could happen for any minute reason, and could last for one day, a month, or longer. During lockdown, every inmate is locked in their cell and must stay on their bunk with no showers. Every day the meals are the same.

- Breakfast—1 boiled egg, prunes, and a box of cold cereal with a pint of milk.
- Lunch—bologna sandwich (no dressing or veggies), and a peanut-butter sandwich with no jelly.
- Dinner—cold chicken patty sandwich (dry), prunes, and a peanut-butter sandwich. All meals come in a brown paper sack.

There is literally no movement—no church—no recreation. After two weeks of that, attitudes get bad, and tempers rise over boiling point. There are fights, which cause the warden to extend the lockdown further punishing the innocent. God used situations like lockdowns to teach me patience. I learned to trust God. I learned to hold my tongue. I learned to let go of the reputation I had and not allow my pride to dictate my attitude in volatile situations. No, prison was not easy, but it was doable with Jesus Christ as my Lord. I learned I had to die daily to my carnal mind, attitude, and actions. I learned to submit my will to the will of God. Every failure and fall in prison was good instruction about life and prepared me for living outside of prison walls again.

I also learned when I willfully sinned; God forgave me and chastised me. But, when I was overtaken by sin, God forgave me with a lesson of wisdom. God is a forgiving God and His forgiving hand was always with divine love or agape love.

Trials are ordained by God. While I was on the Powledge Unit, God taught me how to deal with unbelievers. While on the Jester Unit in Houston, God taught me how to deal with different religions.

The Jester Unit was one of the original units of the prison system, it was also the most dilapidated unit I had ever seen during imprisonment. In the summer it was extra hot and in winter you nearly froze because there was no heat in the buildings. To shower we had to leave the main building, go to another building, and wait in a line outside. This was good in the summer, but in the cold, windy, and sleeting winter months it was a brutal nightmare. The windows in the shower building were broken. Our saving grace during the winter months was that the water was hot. We showered with the cold winter wind howling through the broken window and went outside in thirty degree weather. I endured two winters on the Jester Unit and caught the flu both winters. I prayed it did not turn to pneumonia. God heard and answered my prayer. We had to leave the main building and travel to other buildings for chapel, church, and meals. I questioned the wisdom of God during those times. I thought how could he let this be? Yet, I submitted my will to his will.

Jester was a faith-based unit filled with Baptist, Methodist, and Buddhists. There were a mix of Full Gospel, Pentecostal, and COGIC; along with Church of Christ, Muslims, and Catholics plus any and every other religion in between. I encountered jealousy, pride and spirits of entitlement from the Christian community. They were lessons learned in the fire. I learned I did not have to debate the Word of God; I just had to live His Word.

The Lord had brought me a long way from the 1990's and He was preparing me for release. I did not seek positions; I just was being me, sharing the Word as God lead me to do with my brothers. The Lord blessed me to become a student of His Word and to glorify Him, not to be arrogant and divisive. I attended Bible Study, Sunday Church and chapel services twice a day.

Interchange Freedom was a faith-based program, where we were encouraged to live true to our higher power, but also, how to deal with the problems we would encounter once we were released and mainstreamed back into the free world.

On the Interchange Freedom Unit, 1 of 3 brothers was a preacher—some backsliders, some called while incarcerated. Some were fully committed to Christ, and others had a form of Godliness but did not have the power of the Holy Ghost to sustain them and help them live holy. Not much different from the believer's experience in the free world. Bondage is Bondage. It does not matter if you are behind bars, on lockdown, or walking the sidewalks in the free world held captive by ungodliness—sin.
It is in prison I learned to respect all men, regardless of their religion because God called me to live for Him and not to judge man. In my obedience, the Word living through me will judge others, not me. I was in God's boot camp, He was preparing me for release. I was sixty-two years old. God started me on The Restoration Journey at forty-six years old.

***
Inner Change Freedom Initiative

The Inner Change Freedom Initiative (IFI) was a faith-based re-entry program at the old, out-dated Jester 3 Unit in Richmond, Texas. In preceding pages, I outlined the physical structure of the unit. I would now like to discuss the programs and the people in the programs.

There were 200 men in the program which lasted eighteen months, give or take a few months. Each arriving group was classified as *the next class*. They came from all over Texas Department of Criminal Justice systems. I arrived in March of 2007 and I was in Class 36. Thirty-five classes had come and graduated prior to my arrival. Incoming inmates were housed in the east and west wings with two-man cells built in the 1920's. We stayed in the east and west wing cells until the preceding class graduated, approximately six months. We would then be moved to dorms, which afforded more privacy—a little bit. It was greatly appreciated. The program entailed a series of classes built to bolster one's faith in God and to teach us how to make godly decisions in everyday life.

We all held a four hour job and attended classes when we got off work until nine o'clock at night. A typical day at IFI began with breakfast (4:30 am) and then, Chapel (6:00 – 6:30 AM). After Chapel, we boarded a bus to the Jester 4 Unit of the TDCJ, State Asylum for the Criminal Insane. The inmates were never out of their cells. IFI supplied all the help for this unit, such as Kitchen and laundry workers. We prepared trays for the inmates and delivered them to the cells with officer escorts. We also attended the Officers Dining Room (ODR). My job was in the laundry room.

I arrived, changed into a protective sanitizing suit with mask. I wore long rubber gloves up to my elbow, shoe coverings, and plastic face shield. When the job was done, we had to hose down with a solution and fully shower. It was a filthy job, it was a unit of insane people, but we made it work.
We were back at the unit by eleven o'clock. We showered, ate lunch, and then we began our classes which varied from day to day to make up our required curriculum. After lunch, I had an hour class with our Counselor followed by Toastmasters, N.A, Dinner, Chapel, and then A.A. This was our Monday – Friday routine. Weekends we were free to relax.

The administration gave us permission to have a non-denomination church service on Saturday nights from seven to nine o'clock. The inmates voted in the chapel service under the direction of the IFI program director on the leadership of the Saturday night service, *Breaking of the Bread Service*. Man, oh man, we had some church in the Breaking of the Bread Services.

***
Maturing In Christ

Once Breaking of the Bread Ministry was established and the appointments ratified, the trials began. I knew my appointment was God made and not manmade, even though God went through man to solidify the appointment. Many of the inmates did not feel the same way. They felt since others had been on the unit six to nine months, they should have been given seniority over me. They pleaded with me to abdicate. They cursed me, and even threatened to boycott all the meetings. There were a few men who supported me. Regardless I was focused on getting God's program up and running amid the adversity. I prayed—sought God's guidance, bit my tongue, and denied my flesh.

If the adversity from the men were not enough, I inherited the ministry at the start of the NFL playoffs. I needed a plan to ensure the success of the ministry. First, I called a meeting with the preachers, worked out a rotation schedule, and encouraged them to support each another. Support meant showing up for one another even if a football game was on. Everyone said they were in agreement.

The very first meeting under my leadership went well. The first scheduled brother preached and all the other brothers were in attendance. The next Saturday night, he went to the dayroom to watch football instead of coming to the Breaking of the Bread Church service to support the next brother. I was not quite sure how I was going to handle it, but I did know policing the dayroom on church night was not the answer. I decided to let God handle it. I knew I would be tested before reentry into society, and this was one of those tests.

I was preparing to start the service; when the deacon came to tell me this certain brother was in the dayroom watching football. We walked to the dayroom and I saw with my own eyes the brother watching football. We went back, had a blessed service. The next Saturday night, the errant brother showed up. I stood in front the church and announced he was off the rotation list, and quoted Matthew 7:12—do unto others as you would have them do unto you.

You know how that went over. He and his buddies were hot as you know what. They filed a grievance against me. I got angry, hot and wanted to lash out, but God prevailed. The director, after talking with us both, let the unit know; as the elected overseer, I could do just that. That was how God handled it, and the other ministers supported me. The Lord blessed the Bible study, and my time on the ministry team.

I was baptized in the fire for 18 years in prison, and God's Word had come alive in my life.

I beseech you therefore, brethren, by the mercies of God, that ye present your bodies a living sacrifice, holy, acceptable unto God, which is your reasonable service.

[2] And be not conformed to this world: but be ye transformed by the renewing of your mind, that ye may prove what is that good, and acceptable, and perfect, will of God.

    Romans 12:1-2 KJV

After thirteen years on parole, God is still testing my faith as He did one last time before I would go home.

Breaking of the Bread Ministry was a vital part of each man's life while on the unit because it trained us to serve wherever the Lord would place us upon our release. We were taught the principals of living a godly lifestyle, and to obey those principals. We operated as close to a church as we could; equipped with a choir, deacons, and musicians. We also had ushers along with the scheduled ministers.

Rather than written in books, our greatest lessons learned were engraved in the realities of life. We learned to learned to channel anger, disappointments, and rejection without retaliation. We followed-up on the men when they graduated from IFI and were released into the free world. Unfortunately, the reports were not always good. Some brothers in Christ who did well on the inside, did not fare so well on the outside. They got out and just did not obey, God nor man's laws. Some went back to prison, and some were killed, and I know one for sure is now on death row.

> If we are faithless, He remains faithful; He cannot deny Himself.
> 2nd Timothy 2:13 NKJV

God is yet faithful, even when we are not faithful. I do not know how news of our ill-fated brothers affected others in my class 36, but it affected me sorely. The good reports we received motivated us greatly to be obedient and to remain faithful to our calling. I knew that everything that God allowed in my life was for my spiritual growth

In the program, not only were we getting ready to go back into society, but also we were trained to serve in the Lord's church wherever the Lord placed us after our release. That is where the Breaking of the Bread was so vital in the men life upon their release. We had a choir, deacons, preachers, musicians, and ushers. But, the greatest lessons that we learned was not written in books, but written in the reality of life. When the men graduated from IFI, we kept up with them on the outside. Yes, we learned about the principals of life, but we learned that those principals had to be obeyed more so upon our release. As our brothers in Christ were released, we received some bad reports, because some that did so well on the inside, did not fare so well on the outside. They got out and just did not obey God nor man's law. Some went back to prison, and some were killed, and one I knew for sure is now on death row.

God is yet faithful, even we are not faithful. Now, I do not know how the news like that affected the other men in my group 36, but I started working overtime on me! Also the good reports we received was a great motivator to be obedient. I knew that everything that God allowed in my life was for my spiritual growth. I was learning and yet is learning to deny my fleshly passions and obey the word of God. When I came to IFI on the recommendation of our unit Chaplain at the Powledge Unit (Chaplain William Snidow at the time), I had been in prison 17 years for murder. God was still molding me into the image of His Son Jesus Christ, the year was 2007.

It was time to fill The Breaking of the Bread overseer and Bible study leader positions. Without my knowledge or permission, my name was put in the hat for all the positions named. Back then, I was called "Grandpa", so I tried to be a godly role model for the brothers.

But still, I heard the rumblings of some of the men. Two weeks before graduation, the four nominees were brought before the unit. God blessed me—I was the newly appointed Breaking of the Bread overseer, and co-teacher of the Saturday Morning Bible Study. I did not ask for these positions, God made all that possible, He was in complete control.

I was subject to many trials during that time; sometimes they came because I made decisions in the flesh. All times, God prevailed and worked things out for good.

> [28] And we know that all things work together for good to them that love God, to them who are the called according to his purpose.   Romans 8:28

Reflecting over the years I spent incarcerated, I experienced all the emotions any human being can have; anger, frustration, disappointments, joy, and yes happiness, too. Even with the Lord Jesus in my heart, the road of incarceration is hard. The harness is beneficial in that it allows one to grow in grace and in the knowledge of our Lord Jesus Christ. God allows the school-of-hard-knocks for those whom he loves and has called according to Him whether they or in prison or the free-world. God was preparing me for life outside of prison, and I was well taught.

My parole time was vastly approaching. I had hoped to make parole in January, 2008. It materialized in March, 2008. There was much for Shar'Ron to do. She was commissioned by God to take me back in 1998. She got a place for her to stay because she could not find a place that took ex-cons. Then she found out I would be home in 90 days, she had to find a place that accepted ex-cons. When she did, she had to visit my parole officer and give her the address because I would be on a monitor. The machine had to be at my place of residence. She accomplished all of that.

March 13, 2008 finally arrived. Eight of us were paroled. There was a ritual at IFI for men that are released. It went like this; we gathered in the dayroom, all the men going home that morning, along with a counselor and any inmate who wanted to wish us well. We sat in a circle, received words of encouragement and after an hour or so, we were taken outside the fenced-in compound into a building where we changed from prison clothes into regular clothes. We were then taken to the administration building. One by one the men left the unit. At four o'clock in the afternoon, I was the only one left. My counselor became concerned and called my parole officer in Dallas, who had not let Huntsville know I had been cleared to come home.

When he heard the news; Brother Royce Hall, my brother in Christ who had done time with me, got all the workers at the pickup sight to pray. Counselors were calling and I was getting worried. The secretary told me if Huntsville did not call by five, I would have to go back in and start all over again on Monday—it was Friday.

My heart sank.

"God where are you?" I had to ask.

I waited, I worried, and I watched the clock on the wall. Five minutes to five, the phone rang, and I was cleared to go home.

***
Home

At the last moment I was blessed to get the get out of jail card. Yes, as I watched the office clock, God worked it out. I was escorted to the office building downtown Houston by Mr. Pore, a counselor. My brother in Christ, Royce Hall, picked me up. He drove all the way from Dallas, Texas.

I cannot describe my feelings when I stepped out of the prison compound, to board the shuttle bus. It was surreal. I arrived at the pickup station, greeted Royce, and said my farewells to the workers. Royce and I headed back to Dallas.

"Wanna stop in Houston for burger and fries?" Royce asked. I replied, "I'll wait until we get 50 miles from Dallas before I eat, right now; let us get out of Houston."

It felt so good to be out after eighteen years. I would be on parole for thirteen years.

I was told upon my release I would be on an ankle monitor that was fine with me. I would be double free— free from the power of sin in my life in Christ and free from the physical prison.
Praise the Lord!

As we entered the city limits of Dallas, Royce pointed out to me all the changes that had occurred in the improvements of the city. Royce was talking a hundred words a minute, I don't know who was excited the most, him or me. But, it was all good. Dallas looked very different from the time I left. I gazed at all the changes that had occurred to Dallas. We entered the city and Royce told me where Shar'Ron had gotten an apartment.

Shar'Ron had fixed a homecoming dinner for us. Although God had put Shar'Ron and I back together ten years earlier, I cannot put into words the feeling I had as we pulled up to Shar'Ron's apartment. I was nervous as we approached the apartment.

We knocked on the door, Shar'Ron opened the door, and I embraced her and kissed her. She had prepared a small homecoming dinner for us. That started my journey on the outside, a journey that would only be successful if taken with the Lord Jesus Christ, which was my plan. What was so different about getting out this time from other times was my relationship with Jesus.

JESUS is the difference maker.

I did not crave drinks, drugs, or women. All I wanted was to be used for the service of God. We had a good dinner, laughed and talked for awhile. Royce left, and Shar'Ron and I caught up. Actually, she had not told anyone but our daughter and her sisters what God had done for us. She proceeded to make calls and share the news, I was home. I could not go outside, for they put the monitor on before I left prison and I had to go to orientation the next day.

She did not tell her brothers. People came and Shar'Ron went to South Dallas to pick up my mother and brought her to see me. Remember that my mother and I had a big falling out in 1989. I had not seen my mother in twenty-seven years. My mom walked into the apartment with a walker.

"Now, that is my son." She exclaimed when she saw me. God showed her vision of Jesus in me. Man, it was good to be home, clear headed, sober, and with a sound mind in Christ Jesus.

***
Re-Entry

The following day of freedom was not as heart-felt but still remains endearing to me. It was a commencement of ritual that began with meeting my parole officer. Next there was: getting an ID, making the monitor schedule, and a stiff warning about ex-cons in possession of a firearm. I would be on parole for the next thirteen years. I anticipated there would be trials and setbacks. I was not fearful of what lied ahead of me only because of my faith in God, not because of how strong I thought I was.

Royce was released four years before me and had secured a job at Subway Corporate Office. He secured a job for me at the Subway store on TI Blvd. The job paid $6.25 an hour, thirty-seven hours a week. I started the job less than a week after I was released. I was grateful; the job was a blessing from God. When I got my first pay-check; Shar'Ron took me to the bank to open my very first bank account. I was sixty-four years old.

In the early 1990's haircuts were $10.00, and we used cash and money orders to pay our bills. When I returned home, plastic cards were as valuable as the mean green, and it cost $15.00 to get a haircut. I wish you could have seen me trying to pay for a haircut with a debit card. I was fumbling around with that thing, scratching my head trying to figure out where the money was coming from and how it would get to the barber shop. It was hilarious; the whole barber shop got a laugh on me that day. I just didn't get it.

The first year home was spent getting acclimated to new surroundings. It was a whole new world; I was a sixty-four year old man stumbling around like a lost teen. God kept extending grace, and His helper, Shar'Ron, was tender through the awkward moments. Like when she insisted I get new eyeglasses immediately. She could not stand those prison eyeglasses as she would call them. The eyeglasses and haircut were first on her list.

I had so much to catch up on, cell phones, trains, bus routes, and the changing climate of society in general.

I had to check in with my parole officer weekly to ge get permission and to plan the times I would not be at home so the monitor would not go off and I get a parole violation. It was an adjustment, not to mention they changed the parole officer every six months. I experienced the good, the bad, and the ugly of parole officers. God stayed with me and me with him on the journey.

My job was doing well. Donnie Wilkerson owned the Subway. He was a good boss. I worked there until 2016 when he sold the store. I had my share of trials for my spiritual growth, God is faithful. I rode the bus to the Westmoreland rail station and took the train to work from there. Over the years, I was cursed at, threatened, and bullied. There was a new breed of so called gangsters out there and street life was different from when I had left. I wanted no part of it. I just wanted Christ to be glorified in my life. I did not react to the world's antics the enemy tried to throw at me, rather I acted in the Spirit of Christ.

After being home, for two weeks, I was cleared to go to church from nine am to three pm. The first Sunday, I went with my spiritual mom, Mother Daelene Davis, God's appointed angel of grace to me during my years on the streets. I felt I owed her that for putting up with me when I was in darkness. She was God's constant light in my life of darkness.

***

Moving Forward

On January 12, 2021, I completed thirteen years on parole. I give God all the glory, honor, and credit for this victory.

On the second Sunday, I went to the church Shar'Ron was attending; Evangelist Temple C.O.G.I.C. She had been a member there for thirty years. She had not told the congregation or the Pastor that I was out. No one was expecting me, the long-lost sinner and prisoner to walk through the doors of the church.

All faces were aghast. I marched in with Shar'Ron, Mother Daelene Davis, Brother Royce Hall, and Aunt Helen. It was my personal march of victory. I still believe that was the day I stood my tallest. I felt welcomed and was graciously received. I have been there ever since, allowing God to use me however he saw fit. I was ordained as an Elder in the church, a proud moment of victory for me. There I was blessed to do prison ministry along with my wife, Sister Triena Dabney, and Brother Eddie Griffin. We started the prison Ministry in 2015 and continued faithfully until the Pandemic closed the prison's doors in 2020.

After I was laid-off from Subway, I was referred to Miles of Freedom; a non-profit organization at the MLK Community Center in South Dallas. This referral came as a result of Shar'Ron's endless support and sharing my testimony when and wherever God led her to do so. It turned out to be very helpful. I would not be typing this story on my computer if it had not been for the Miles of
Freedom program.

Once enrolled in the program, I had to attend a ninety-day workshop. After graduation, they worked with clients to meet our basic needs, especially those coming out of prison and in addiction recovery. One day, I was talking to the administrator, Mrs. Tahvia Merrill, who encouraged me to go to East Field College and major in Health Science to become a Licensed Chemical Dependency Counselor (LDCD).

I did not know how to turn on a computer, much less than use one. Mrs. Merrill assured me it would be easy, and she would tutor me. I enrolled in a class, and met with Mrs. Merrill once a week for computer class.

In May, 2019 I graduated with a certificate in Substance Abuse Counseling. I took my internship at the Salvation Army Therapeutic Center in Dallas. I was a natural because parolees, and those ordered by the court for rehab were the clients. I understood them better than the veteran counselors because I had traveled the very road they were on. I was asked to return after I applied for licensing with the State of Texas. I was excited about my chance to make some real money, bless my wife and to be a significant help to someone else.

I finished my internship, sent the paperwork to Austin, and waited for my license. My classmates were getting their papers and getting good jobs. After two months, I called Austin to find out the status of my application. I was told my application for counselor was denied, and they would send a letter to explain.

The letter came and I was informed I could not be licensed in Texas to Counsel because of my record. I have a 1st degree murder case which was at the time twenty-five years ago. I felt as if I had been punched in the gut. What could I do? I am over seventy years old, with the usual old age aches and pain. I did not know what I was going to do, but I did know God was still in control of my life.

Here I am, in the middle of a Global Pandemic, preaching on facebook every evening, and still in school. I don't know what my future holds, but I do know who holds my future. My educational advisor at East Field, Mrs. Alexi Calhoun encouraged me to write my journey and so you have read. It is all to God's Glory.

I pray my story inspires you or someone you know to believe in God's Amazing Grace and His power to save all who are lost. I heard about it—I experienced it—and I now live it. How about you? Jesus is waiting.

About The Author

Evangelist Kenneth Morey James is the founder of The Amazing Grace Evangelistic Crusades Prison Ministry originally founded at the Powledge Unit in Palestine, Texas. He holds an Associate Degree in Substance Abuse Counseling. He is committed to a life of servitude to Jesus Christ and to all who he encounters along his journey. His passion is for those in need of direction, hope, and salvation as they transition from imprisonment and addiction.

He has excelled in the evangelistic ministry and is deeply rooted in the Word of God. He particularly enjoys training the next generation of leaders in the body of Christ.

He is a strong mentor, motivator and inspirational speaker whose life experiences and love for Jesus Christ are a true testament of God's redeeming power and love for us all.

Evangelist James believes family is the core of life and a happy family is necessary for a successful ministry. A native of Dallas, Texas he and wife, Shar'Ron reside with daughter Valeicyia in the DFW area. They enjoy spending time together with family, friends, children, grandchildren and great-grandchild.

Evangelist James is available for ministry, mentoring, and motivational speaking. He and his wife Shar'Ron are available for marriage Seminars.

Contact:
 Evangelist James 469-235-9411
Sister Shar'ron James 469-733-5603
Email: www.kennethmoreyjames.com

This Is Us

Made in the USA
Columbia, SC
09 October 2022